Bass F Scratch

Is this the right book for you, Young Bassist?

Here's what you'll find:

- Practical tips to get you up and playing the bass as soon as possible
- An easy pace that will keep you engaged and won't leave you behind
- A straightforward narrative that connects the dots (no quantum leaps)
- Plenty of song examples from popular music that you'll recognize
- Just enough theory to affirm that you know what you are doing
- Tablature and Fretboard Diagrams for expeditious learning
- Always the chance to skip ahead to something easier

Here's what you WON'T find:

Standard music notation, which can
bog down even the most intrepid student.

Instruction on how to create your own melodic basslines.
Best to learn backup first and become a reliable accompanist.

Free Audio Files at www.SkepticalGuitarist.com

Other Titles by **Bruce Emery**:

Guitar From Scratch series
Guitar From Scratch
Guitar From Scratch: The **Sequel**
Fingerstyle Guitar From Scratch
Blues Guitar From Scratch
Travis-Style Guitar From Scratch
Guitar From Scratch: **Streamlined Edition**

Music Principles for the Skeptical Guitarist series:
Volume One: The Big Picture
Volume Two: The Fretboard
Jazz for the Skeptical Guitarist

Ukulele From Scratch
Baritone Ukulele From Scratch
Mandolin From Scratch

Christmas Carol series:
Christmas Strumalong Guitar
Christmas Fingerstyle Guitar
Ukulele Christmas Carols
Mandolin Christmas Carols

More info at: **www.SkepticalGuitarist.com**

Bass From Scratch

by

Bruce Emery

Skeptical Guitarist Publications

© Copyright 2014 Skeptical Guitarist Publications

All rights reserved.

Manufactured in the United States of America

ISBN: 978-0-9788609-7-7

Cover design: Marc Harkness <marc@marcharkness.net>

Webmaster: Lou Dalmaso <loudalmaso@att.net>

Skeptical Guitarist Publications
Post Office Box 5824
Raleigh, NC 27650-5824
(919) 834-2031

Web site: www.SkepticalGuitarist.com

Find audio files and an e-mail link

First Edition

Acknowledgments

To my editors and advisers: Sue Scott, Katherine Polk, Bill Erchul and Jill Soha
Thanks for the Fender J-Bass, Bill.....oh, did you want it back?

Table of Contents

Compelling Introduction 1
Points of Order 2
Layout of the Bass and Tuning 3

Here We Go 4
Keeping the Beat 7
Classic Rock Groove 8
Relative Tuning 9
The Root and the Octave 10
Adding the 5th 12
Root, 5th and Octave 14

Chords, Chords, Chords 16
1 - 4 - 5 System in the Key of A 17
Other *CAGED* Keys 18
1 - 4 - 5 Examples 21
The 5 Chord Versus the 5th Degree 24

Triads 26
1 - 4 - 5 Examples with 1 - 3 - 5 Triads 27
Value of the 3rd in the Triad 31
Adding the 6th: Boogie-Woogie

The Major Scale 34
C Major Scale 36
Other Major Scales 38
Purpose of Major Scales in Basslines 41
Examples of Passing Tones 42

Minor Chords in Chord Families 47
2m Chord and the Rhythm Changes 56
3m Chord 58

Circle of Fifths 59
Examples 62
Morning Has Broken 64

Flatted Seventh Degree 66
Box Pattern 67
Examples 67

Swing Time 70

Boogie With the Flatted Seventh 71
Movable Boogie Pattern 72
Examples 72

Blues and Rock 74
Minor Pentatonic Scale 75
Examples 76
Chord Changes in the Blues 79

Minor Keys 81
A Minor Chord Family 82
Flamenco Chord Progression 85

Clave Rhythm: Bo Diddley Beat 86

What Readers of My Other Books Have to Say

Emery is a teacher who apparently has ESP when it comes to learning guitar. Things are broken down into such sensible pieces that you'll wonder why everybody doesn't teach this way. *Recommended!*
Elderly Instruments, Lansing, MI

Thank you for writing something intelligent and witty, something I actually looked forward to reading. Eternal gratitude.
Meredith Cox, Raleigh, NC

I bought your book because it made me laugh.
Mike Schwartz, Montclair, NJ

Send more books! Our customers are eating them like peanuts.
Linda Tillman, McFadyen Music, Fayetteville, NC

Thanks for your warm and friendly style and bits of humorous illustration.
George Demosthenes, New Market, NH

Focused and vastly readable... Conversational approach is warm and engaging...Humor, insight and patience.
David McCarty, Acoustic Guitar Magazine

You are a miracle worker. I'm having the time of my life.
Chuck Slaughter, Cyberspace

The books sell themselves.
David Willmott, Music-Go-Round, Cary, NC

It's written just like you're sitting there teaching me.
Barrett Ferrara, Cyberspace

Your writing is breezy and conversational but still very clear and organized.
Chris Gaskill, Knoxville, TN

You clearly have a real gift, and we're lucky that you put it down on paper
Mark Waite. Houston, TX

There is no better teaching aid on the market than your books. You could write a book on the proper way to put a guitar on a guitar stand and I would buy it! **Kevin Johnson, San Antonio, TX**

The format is easy on the eyes. Bruce writes in a clear and understandable manner, making it fun to learn.
Ed Benson, Just Jazz Guitar magazine

If you write it, they will buy it.
Paul Miller, New Bern, NC

Bruce, this is an absolutely terrific book. It shows that you have a wonderful sense of humor, a high degree of humility and a great sensitivity to others. A++ and many kudos.
Dick Masom, Tequesta, FL

Bruce Emery has "got it right" with his gentle pace.
Adrian Ingram, Just Jazz Guitar magazine

I can see why people raved about this. This is a great thing you did.
Thomas McLachlen, Pittsburgh, PA

Your content is golden.
Marko Schmitt, Cyberspace

Thanks for getting me fired up! I can play more in 4 weeks than I could after all those years of trying to teach myself.
Kim Lachance, Dover, NH

Your books are greatness because of the enjoyment you experienced while writing them. I was instantly won over by your wit.
Christian Briere, Weatherford, TX

Enjoyable to read; short, to the point and jam-packed full of information.
Lynn Sugg, Winterville, NC

All I can say is YES! Someone has finally hit the nail on the head.
Martin Bell, Staffordshire, England

A Compelling Introduction

I've been a **bass** since high school. No, not the fish. A second bass
in the Concert Choir. When my voice dropped, it just kept on dropping.

Most of Our Music is chordal. A **chord** is a vertical stack of **tones** that blend together,
more or less, into a pleasing aural experience. These **notes** range from lower **pitches** to
higher pitches that all people (probably most animals, some houseplants) can distinguish.

In choir, the highest vocal part is the **soprano**, which is often where the **melody** resides.
The melody is the most important musical line there is, and it's best to have it on the top
of the pile where it can stand out and be heard most easily. Not buried in the middle.

Next down is the **alto** part, which is mostly responsible for a **harmony** line,
a set of notes that is usually not as strong as the melody, but beautifully supportive.
The **tenor** part can provide yet a lower harmony line, and as the highest male part,
it will also handle the melody line, especially in an all-male chorus.

Then. Deep in the muck, at the bottom of the ocean floor, resides the **bass**. (Resisting
another fish joke.) The bass's job is to provide a bottom, a sturdy platform that can take
the weight of all the parts above it. We provide the bed that everyone else sleeps on.

Sometimes the bass will take the melody or a harmony line, but that's usually for
the sake of variety. It isn't long before we are sent back down to the basement
to shovel more coal into the furnace.

The bass guitarist is considered to be half guitarist, half drummer, with perhaps
more emphasis on the drumming side, because the bass plays a huge **rhythmic** role
in keeping the beat, establishing the groove and moving the music forward.

But I suspect that many people come to the bass from the **guitar**, as I did.
And I'll bet that most of these people are interested in broadening their abilities
so that they can play a supporting role in small folk-rock-country or church
ensembles that sport too many guitarists as it is, all champing at the bit.

So I'm going to keep the guitar in mind as we explore the lower reaches
of the Musical Universe. Welcome to the boom boom room.

Points of Order

When the Beatles formed, it was decided (probably by John Lennon, yeah?) that Paul McCartney would play the bass because George Harrison was better at playing the guitar. Word is that Paul wasn't too keen on the idea at first because playing bass was considered to be a yawn. But Paul McCartney decided to EXPLODE that stereotype and *to play the bass as if it were a guitar*. We'll get to that, but let's start playing the bass as if it were a bass.

First see what fun sounds we can make before we dig in and learn about scales, arpeggios and grooves.

Several Points of Order:

(1) *You won't be learning to read music.* You won't use it. If you ever *do* need it, say if you wind up playing in jazz ensembles or orchestra pits, you can learn it **then**. Remember, I'm figuring on the folk-rock-country-praise musician, not the jazz guy.

In this book, the notes you'll play will be shown in **Tablature (Tab)** and **Fretboard Diagrams**, which are pretty easy to interpret. My main concern here is to get you *playing*. Starting with "the clefs and the dots and the beams" would bring things to a grinding halt.

(2) *You WILL need to learn the names of the notes on the neck of the bass*; well, you'll start by memorizing the locations of some of the most useful notes, such as the **A** note at the 5th fret of the **E** string, and then you'll be able to fill in the rest, such as the **A-sharp** note at the *6th fret*. But this is a critical skill to develop.

(3) *You are welcome to play either pickstyle or fingerstyle.* Most other bass books I've seen emphasize playing fingerstyle right away, which is fine, but it has a pretty steep learning curve, especially if you intend to use the commonly accepted technique, where you try to alternate your Index and Middle fingers in striking the strings. Of course, the great Rhythm & Blues bassist, James Jamerson, used only his Index finger, and the first electric bass players in the Fifties played with their thumbs.

Pickstyle playing is more commonly used in rock and folk music because it gives a better punch, more articulation. Besides, most recreational guitarists already know how to use a pick to perform simple Downstrokes and Upstrokes.

First let's focus more on the concerns of the *left hand*, which are to learn to finger the notes and scales and riffs and licks, and less on the mechanics of the right hand.

BTW, if you do use a pick, make it a heavier gauge.

The Layout of the Bass and How to Tuna

Behold below, a *killer* diagram of the bass that even looks something *like* a bass, since all the salient features can *almost* be discerned. You have the **headstock**, which houses the 4 **tuners** where the strings are attached. The **strings** pass through grooves in the **nut**, down the **fretboard** and across the **frets**. That's the **neck**. Then the **body** has the **pickups**, which capture the sound vibrations; the **bridge**, where the strings are attached; and the **control knobs** that work the volume (hi/lo) and tone (bass/treble).

Then there is a **strap pin** and an **end pin** for attaching a strap (probably a good idea whether you will be standing or sitting to play) and an **input jack** where you plug in.

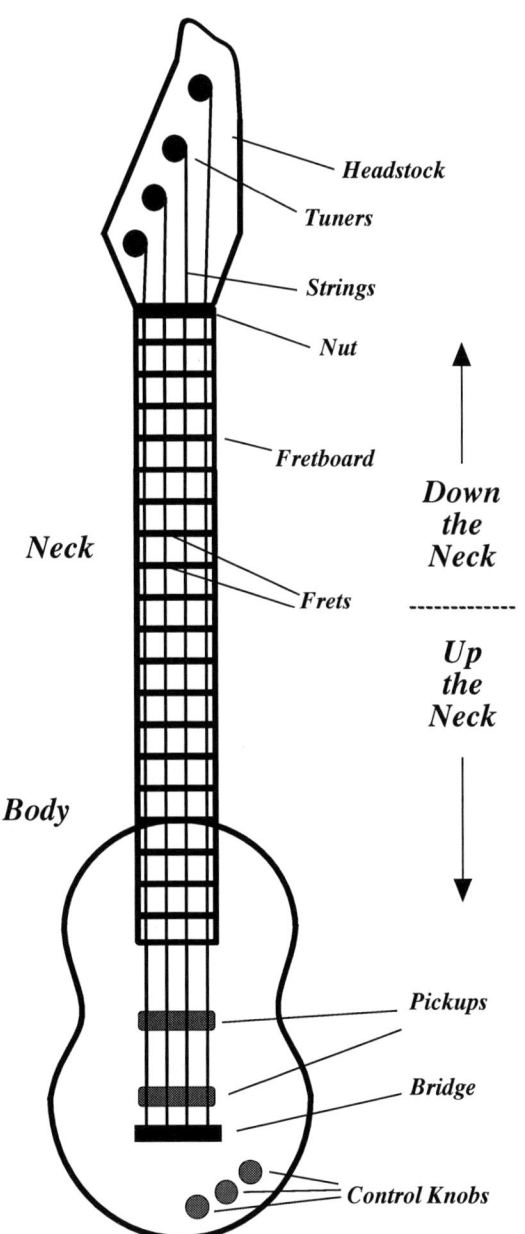

So, pretty much just a big guitar with a couple of strings missing, right? And you just play one note at a time? How hard can it be to play?

Well. While having guitar experience does give a leg up on playing the bass, it does *not* prepare you for the extra *physical effort* needed to do the job.

The bass is heavier, the strings are thicker and the frets are farther apart. Flat-wound strings are easier on your fingertips, but the round-wound strings are cheaper and brighter-sounding (though brightness is often a disadvantage.....)

You will need to develop some extra strength and flexibility to play the bass, ***So Don't Rush It!***

It's easy to strain your left arm particularly, ***So Go Slow!***

The GOOD news is that **Tuning the Bass** won't be *too* problematic, especially if you have the foresight to acquire an **electronic tuner**. (If you're a guitarist, you probably already have one of these gizmos.)

So get the Gang at the Music Store to sell you one and teach you how to use it (it's all visual and easy to handle) and I'll show you the process of **Relative Tuning** later, after you've messed around with your bass a bit.

Here We Go

So, I am assuming you have access to a bass, or know how to contact a music store to get one. I have no opinion on the *kind* of bass you should learn on, just that it works. You know, the strings shouldn't be too far from the fretboard, and of course you need an amplifier, which the same Gang can help you with. Wouldn't hurt to take along a knowledgeable friend, though. Maybe a tall, scary one.

I understand that ***The Inner Game of Tennis***, written by Timothy Gallway in 1974, suggested that people just go out and the hit the ball around in the beginning, to get a feel for the game before engaging in the analytical process. Should work for bass as well.

Still, we need some form of music notation. On the guitar there are 6 strings that are numbered 1 through 6, but **on the bass there are 4 strings that aren't really numbered.** What is up with that? The strings are called the **E, A, D** and **G** strings, from low to high.

One possible reason: The guitarist recognizes that **E, A, D** and **G** are the names of the *6th, 5th, 4th and 3rd strings*, but on the bass they'd be the *4th, 3rd, 2nd and 1st strings*, so the numbers might serve only to confuse guitarists. But I feel like being inclusive, so we'll call the strings the **E/4th, A/3rd, D/2nd** and **G/1st** strings. No confusion.

On the left is a Fretboard Diagram and on the right is a Tab Diagram:

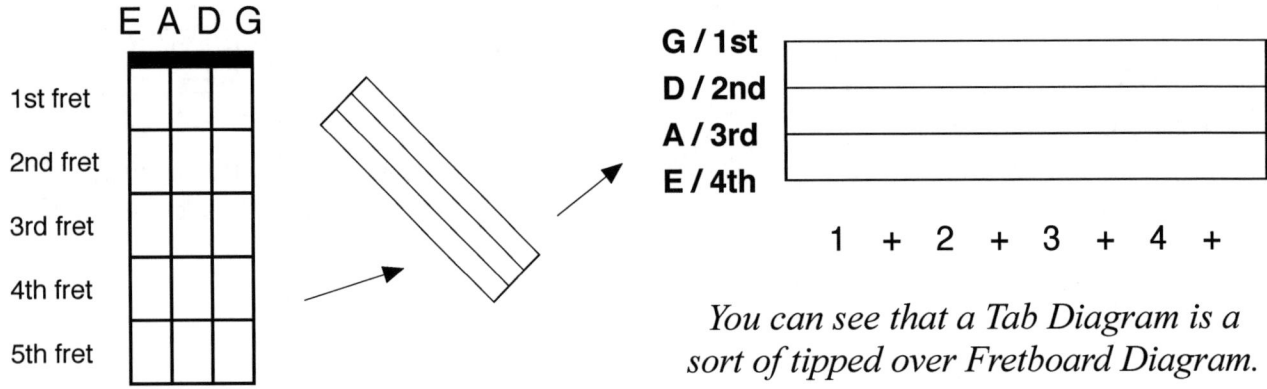

You can see that a Tab Diagram is a sort of tipped over Fretboard Diagram.

Why do we need both? Well, the Fretboard Diagram pinpoints the locations of notes on the neck; it's pictorial. Those are the **frets** going *across* and the **strings** going *up and down*. (This Fretboard Diagram goes up to the 5th fret, and we call it "up the neck" because *pitch increases as you go **down** the page*, from the nut to the bridge.)

But it tells you nothing about either the passage of time or the sequence of notes. The Tab Diagram shows 4 **beats** or **counts** of music and the half beats in between, and that's **one measure** or **bar** of what we call **4/4 Time**, or 4 counts to the bar.

Okay, sit down, put your bass in your lap, strap it on, switch it on, and tune it up. Play the open **4th** string, the **E** string, the one closest to your face, the lowest in pitch, **4 times** while counting **1 - 2 - 3 - 4**. Your left hand is just cradling the neck.

Here's what you just did, expressed in Tab:

Remember, the lowest line depicts the lowest note in *pitch*, but that's the highest string in *elevation*.

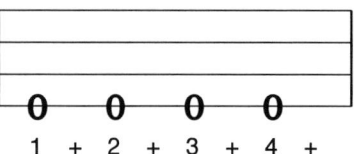

So that's one measure or bar of **4/4 Time**. 4/4 is known as the **Time Signature** for this measure of music. The top "4" refers to the 4 beats. The bottom "4" tells you that the **note value** for each of those 4 notes is the **Quarter-note**, or 1/4 of the measure. (We'll also be playing Eighth-notes, Half-notes and Whole-notes, and you can guess what portion of a measure each one of *those* notes consumes.)

I suppose the next item on our to-do list is to try the same thing on the other 3 strings:

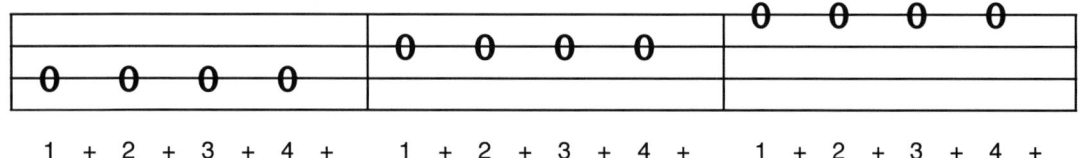

If you're using a pick, and I kinda hope you are, you can play all **Downstrokes (D D D D)** or you can alternate Downstrokes with **Upstrokes (D U D U)**. Probably not all Upstrokes. All Downstrokes is stronger, but whether you do all Downs or alternate is up to you.

Passages that need more speed might benefit from alternation; notice that your hand has to travel down and up *twice as many times* if you do all Downstrokes.

If you're even a little curious about *fingerstyle playing*, here's one way to do it.

For the E/4th string, plant your thumb on the pickup nearest the neck and alternate your Index and Middle fingers to play those 4 notes, starting with either finger. These will be **rest strokes**, where you "ram" the fingers into the planted thumb, using it as a brake.

For the other 3 strings, plant your thumb on the **E/4th** string.

When you play the **A/3rd** string, the thumb again acts as a brake.
When you play the **D/2nd** string, the **A** string acts as a brake.
When you play the **G/1st** string, the **D** string acts as a brake.

Try it. Most bassists can play with either pick or fingers.

Well, we won't get very far without doing some fretting. Play the open **E/4th** string, then place your *1st finger at the 1st fret* and press down. Press harder. *Harder!* If you get a buzzing sound, you need to press even harder, and it's best to situate the tip of your finger as close to the 1st fret *wire* as possible; you'll get a better purchase on it, and a better chance of getting a clean sound.

Here's your first song. You *should* recognize it, but I won't tell you what it is yet. Let it suffice to say that it's the theme music from a movie about a jolly big fish (no, not a bass). You'll simply be alternating the two notes; count them out:

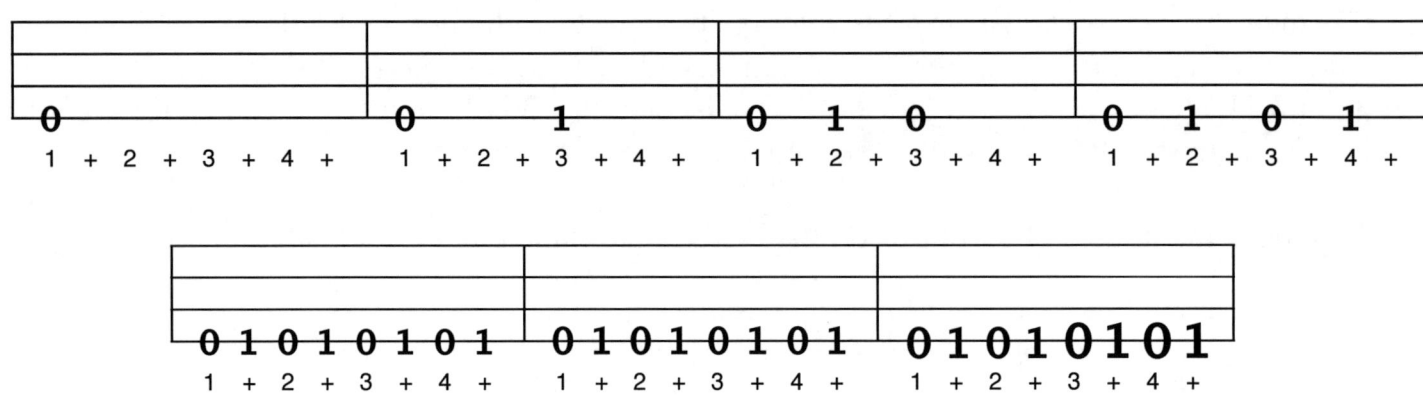

I don't expect you to get that 2nd line up to speed just yet, but it *is* kind of ominous, right? That, of course, is the theme to the 1975 Oscar-winning thriller, *"What's New, Pussycat?"* Or was it *"Jaws"*? That's it, *"What's New, Jaws?"* (Try this on the 3 other strings, too.)

The first bar contains one note, the **E** note, and it gets the note value of a **Whole-note**. Takes up the whole measure. The second bar contains 2 **Half-notes**, **E** again, *and now F*. Just like the alphabet! The Musical Alphabet is **ABCDEFG** and starts over with **A**. And notice how I use the terms "bar" and "measure" interchangeably. So can you.

The 3rd measure contains 2 Quarter-notes and a Half-note (**E-F-E**), and the 4th measure has 4 Quarter-notes (**E-F-E-F**). Then the entire last line is full of **Eighth-notes**; you can alternate Down- and Upstrokes, although all Downstrokes *would* be more menacing.

Remember, your job is to be a human metronome, keeping the time, providing a rallying point for all the other musicians present. Don't worry so much about the Eighth-notes right now, but be sure that you're playing the Quarter-notes *dead evenly*, either **D D D D** or **D U D U**. *Boy, a metronome would come in mighty handy (hint).*

In fact, our next section is all about.......

Keeping the Beat: The First Dimension

We start with the beat-keeping, rhythmic function of the bass, so let's put aside the fretted notes for now and just play open strings. (Changing notes on a string to create melodic and harmonic interest will consitute the Second Dimension.)

About the *least* you can play is **one note per measure.** Here's how it looks on the 4 strings:

```
|---------------|---------------|---------------|------0--------|
|---------------|---------------|------0--------|---------------|
|---------------|------0--------|---------------|---------------|
|--0------------|---------------|---------------|---------------|
  1 + 2 + 3 + 4 +   1 + 2 + 3 + 4 +   1 + 2 + 3 + 4 +   1 + 2 + 3 + 4 +
```

May seem silly, but try counting out loud the "**1** and **2** and **3** and **4** and." Count it *e-v-e-n-l-y*.

But is this Whole-note pattern very common? Sure, in a slower ballad, or in a song where you want to start out more relaxed, and then build the intensity by adding more notes to each bar. At the other end of the spectrum, for maximum intensity, you could use all **8 Eighth-notes**:

```
|---------------|---------------|---------------|--0 0 0 0 0 0 0 0--|
|---------------|---------------|--0 0 0 0 0 0 0 0--|---------------|
|---------------|--0 0 0 0 0 0 0 0--|---------------|---------------|
|--0 0 0 0 0 0 0 0--|---------------|---------------|---------------|
  1 + 2 + 3 + 4 +   1 + 2 + 3 + 4 +   1 + 2 + 3 + 4 +   1 + 2 + 3 + 4 +
```

But we'll spend most of our time somewhere in the middle. Now I want to draw you into playing the **Classic Rock Groove**, but I want to get there in several steps, because it can be a bit tricky. Try it on the **A/3rd** string (try the others later), starting with *4 Quarter-notes*:

This is at a medium intensity, and you do need to get good at playing groups of 4 steady beats, so go ahead and play this over and over, *trying to give a bit more emphasis to **Count 1***: But I will admit that it's rather dry and repetitive. Now...

Add an *Eighth-note* at **Count 2+**: *one - two-**and** - three - four*. If you're picking both Downs and Ups, try going: **D DUD D**. Play the bar, then loop it around and start over at *one* again.

Next, lose the note at **Count 4**. What do we have now? One quarter-note, two eighth-notes and a half-note, which is certainly making things more interesting, but it's still feels on the *square* side of things. Still a bit *marchy*. (Let the half-note on **Count 3** ring on for *two entire beats* before starting over.)

So let's hip it up a bit. *Remove the Eighth-note* on **Count 2**: This is the Classic Rock Groove. Embrace it and rejoice!

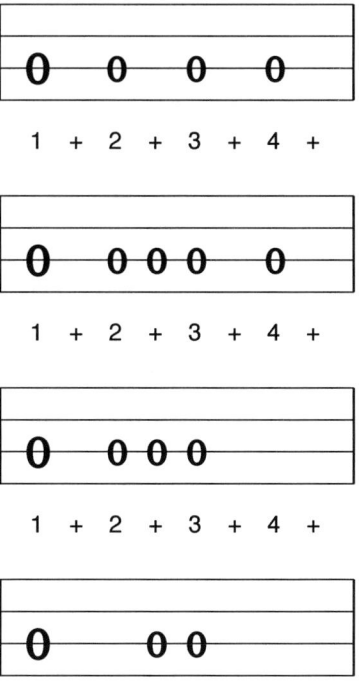

The Classic Rock Groove

Try alternating one measure of this pattern on the **A/3rd** string with one measure on the **D/2nd** string. Almost sounds like music! (Say "**2**" but don't *play* until "**and.**")

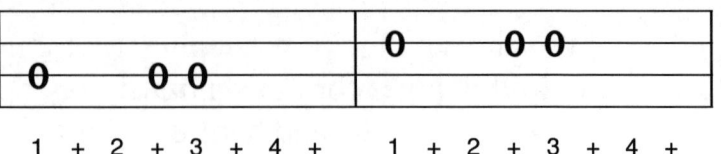

A **groove** is a rhythmic pattern that repeats throughout a song over most chord changes. The key feature of this groove, the funky part of it, is *the gap between the first two notes*. It's as if we took the original Quarter-note from **Count 2** and pushed it *one half-beat later* without postponing the 3rd note at all. That's the tricky part. Sort of, wait, then hurry up. *Try not to take away from the dominance of the 1st note by playing the 2nd note too early.* Then, be sure to play the 3rd note **right on the beat**. Count: **1 - (2) and-3** (let it ring).

This is why you need to *keep counting*, either with a metronome or the metronome in your head, and keep track of where the **numbered counts** are, the **1**, the **2**, the **3** and the **4**. These beats are like four tent-poles that hold up the measure, or four equally spaced bus stops where the buses must always arrive exactly on time, *whether or not anyone gets on or off.*

The "**and**" counts between the numbered counts are weaker and less distinct, so when the numbered counts start being omitted, the entire structure can get very wobbly.

But I'll tell you what. The management of the "**and**" counts will be the key to your success.

Muting the Strings

So far, we've just been hitting the strings and letting them ring until we hit them again. But it's also possible to **damp** them, or mute them out, before the next note comes along. You can stop the vibration early by *touching* the string with the left- or right-hand fingers, or with the pick. (With *fretted* strings, left-hand muting is best: you can just release the pressure on the note *without* letting go of the string, and the vibration dies forthwith.)

Play the note on **Count 1**, and bring the fingers of your left hand down onto the ringing string right on **Count 2**. Don't press, just touch.

Then *immediately* play the notes at **Count 2+** and **Count 3**, in quick succession and mute the ringing string *again* at **Count 4**. This gives a crisper, more rhythmic effect. (And it leaves room for a drummer to hit the snare drum, or a guitarist to play the "chick" of a "boom-chick" strum pattern, on **Counts 2** and **4**.)

You now have enough RHYTHMIC knowledge of the bass to competently back up any recreational musical group!

Relative Tuning

This is as good a time as any to describe the process of **Relative Tuning**, where you use a note from one string as a standard for tuning an adjacent string. I suppose you've acquired, and are employing, an electronic tuner, but sometimes they get misplaced or the battery dies, and then where are you? You're up Bass Creek without a paddle, my little minnow.

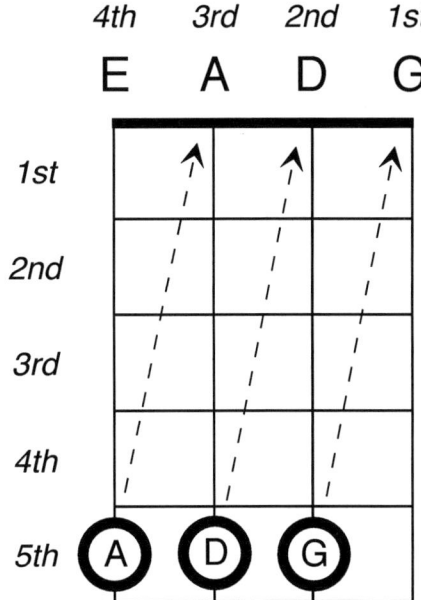

All right, let's start with the **G/1st** string.

You'll need to procure a standard **G** note from a reliable source, such as a pitch pipe or a keyboard, to compare with the current pitch of your **G** string. If one of these is not available, heck with it, just assume that your **G** string is on the money.

It just so happens that the note at the 5th fret of the **D/2nd** string is also supposed to be a **G** note; in fact, it should have the very same, **unison** pitch (Unison = one sound). They should sound *just alike*. And they probably are *already* pretty close, unless any children or banjo players have been around.....

Play the D string at the 5th fret, keep it ringing, and add the sound of the open G string. This is where **perfect pitch** comes in. Now, this is very important. **Perfect pitch** is when you throw a banjo into a Dumpster and it hits another banjo. Or a button accordion. (I don't know why I'm picking on banjos and accordions; I love 'em both.)

No, actually, perfect pitch is not the issue here, it's **relative pitch**. If we can get these two **G** notes into unison, then we've tuned one string *relative* to the other.

So get them ringing. If they're close but not *in* tune, you'll hear a wavering sound, a sort of "*wawawawa*." Your job is to make that beating sound disappear, by turning one of the tuning pegs one way or the other. Which peg? Remember, the open **G** is the standard, so don't turn that one! Pick a direction and turn the **D** string peg. If the "*wawa*" gets *faster*, oops, wrong way, go back t'other way. You want it to get slower and slower until the "*waaawaaawaaa*" becomes "*waaaaaaa*."

Once that happens, you're in tune. Then apply the same process to get the **A** string in tune with the **D** string, then the **E** string in tune with the **A** string, according to the diagram above.

Once a bass is in tune, it won't vary by much unless you knock it. But it sure is nice to have an electronic tuner on board to help you with those small occasional tweakings.

The Root and the Octave

I'd like to start introducing tiny bits of technique and music theory side by side; start knocking the tennis ball up against the wall to see how it bounces.....and why.

Consider one note, the **A** note, on the open 3rd string. The playing we're about to do will center on the **A** note, the **Root Note** of a **scale**. This scale will contain other notes as well, but the **A** note will stand out as The Boss, as we usually start and stop our musical phrases playing the **Root** and generally drop by there more frequently.

There are other A notes lurking about, such as the **unison A** note you just played at the 5th fret of the **E/4th** string (Relative Tuning). *More importantly, there is an A note at the 2nd fret of the G/1st string that is one OCTAVE higher in pitch than the others.*

Here are a Tab and a Fretboard Diagram of the open **A** note and its octave:

The term octave comes from "octo," meaning "eight." The two **A** notes are said to be an octave apart because the 8 steps in the old *Do-Re-Mi* scale connect them. Here's this scale over the length of the **A** string:

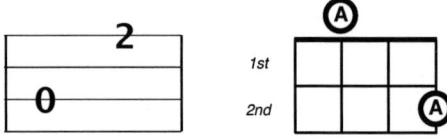

Everyone knows the **Do-Re-Mi** scale, (*Sound of Music*), better known as the **Major Scale**, and we'll dig more into it over the course of the book.

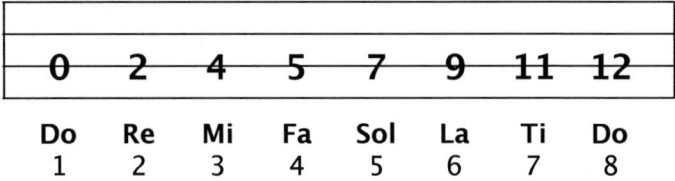

*Definition: The **A Major Scale** and its associated chords belong to the **Key of A**.*

Go ahead and play these 8 notes up the **A** string, and when you hit the 12th fret, compare that high **Do** with the low **Do**. Notice how they sound......*alike*.....but *not*. Dumb as it seems, this may be the best way to define an octave. One **A** note is high and the other is low, but they blend perfectly. Something to do with frequencies.

Now play the 2nd fret of the **G/1st** string. *Sounds just like that 12th fret note*; in fact, it's a unison **A** note, and it will be a lot handier for us to play the one down the neck.

On the next page, there are some examples of how Actual Bassists have applied the **Root Note** and its **Octave**. As we go along, I'll refer to plenty of popular songs to illustrate the workings of the bass, so you can scoot over to YouTube to hear them. They've been simplified, and usually you won't hear them in the original keys, but most riffs work in all keys. BTW, a **riff** (slang for "rhythm figure") is just a short, repeated musical phrase. Pop music is dripping with them.

So give these a try, either pickstyle or fingerstyle. We're playing in what is called **Open Position** because of the presence of the open string. *You can repeat the music between the heavier bar lines as many times as you like.* And you can use your 2nd finger to hold down that Octave **A**:

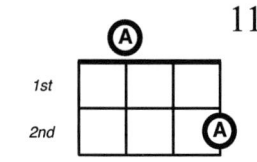

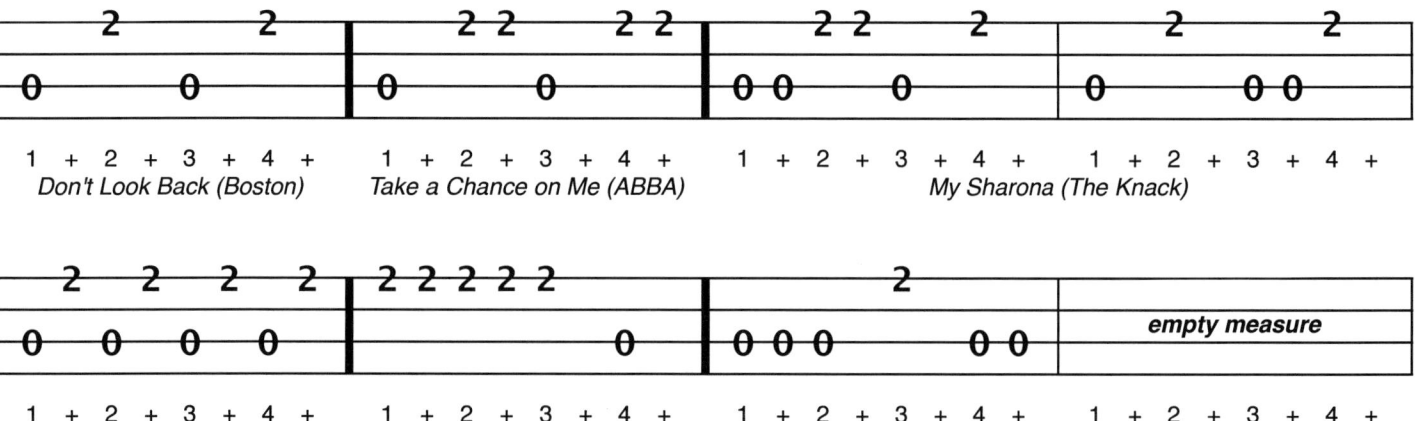

Don't be concerned with speed right now; just keep the beat e-v-e-n and count out loud.

Are you noticing a problem with the open strings? *They just keep on **ringing**!* Often, that's not what you'd prefer. It's better when these deep, booming bass notes aren't permitted to ring into each other. Muddy! It's not an issue with the fretted notes: Just release the pressure, without letting go of the string. But oh, those open notes.....

It's far better to damp them, mute them, cut them somehow or other, with some finger. OR.....You can do the *manly* thing, and run away. This the path I bravely recommend.

Go grab that **A** note at the 5th fret of the **E/4th** string that is in unison with the open **A**. Now, there's a *fretted* note you can control! But to play those riffs, how would you reach from the 5th fret all the way down to the 2nd fret to play the octave? Oh.....you cheat.

From what you know about Relative Tuning, you can suppose that *most notes on the bass have **a unison note 5 frets higher** on the **next lower (in pitch) string***. So the **A** note on the 1st string has a unison note on the 7th fret of the 2nd string. Try those riffs again, in **5th Position**:

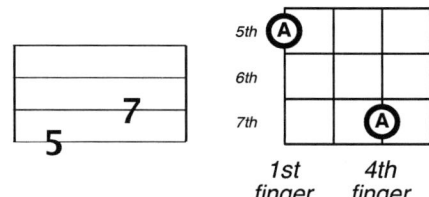

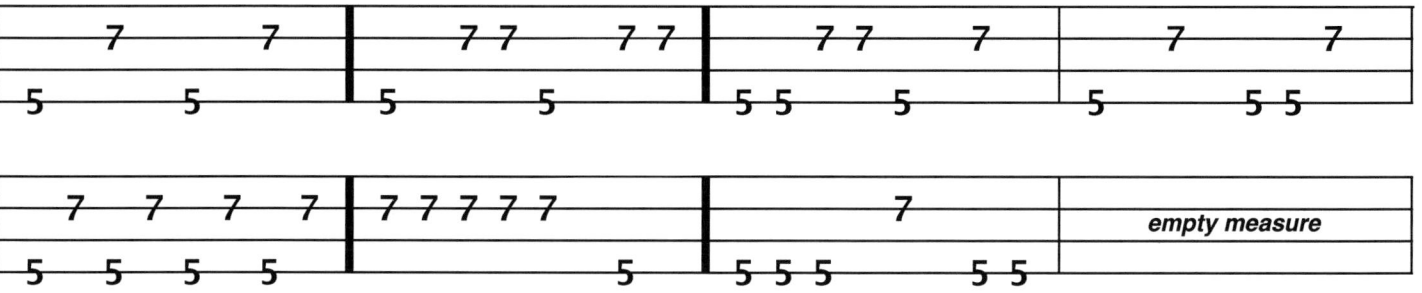

5th Position means that the *1st finger* plays the note at the *5th fret.*
Try the 4th finger at the 7th fret.

Now I can control the "sustain" on all my notes. I can let them ring for a more flowing, connected feeling, or I can cut them off short for a more percussive, staccato feeling.

What I give up by avoiding open strings is a brief, tiny alleviation of fatigue every time I *don't* need to press down on the string to get a note, and those pauses do accumulate and help to mitigate arm pain early on. So there's your trade-off. In the long run, you'll probably play open strings mostly when you *have* to.

Adding the 5th

Well, that was fun. But we're just getting *started* taking other notes from the scale to come up with interesting riffs. Technically, we haven't started *yet*, because the **Root** and the **Octave** (also known as the **8th degree** of the scale) are effectively the same note, and adding the **8th** contributes no harmonic variety.

But adding the **5th degree** *does*. The **5th** is the second most important note in the Major Scale, and has everything to do with the **Circle of Fifths**, the engine that drives much of our Western music from one chord to another. More later.

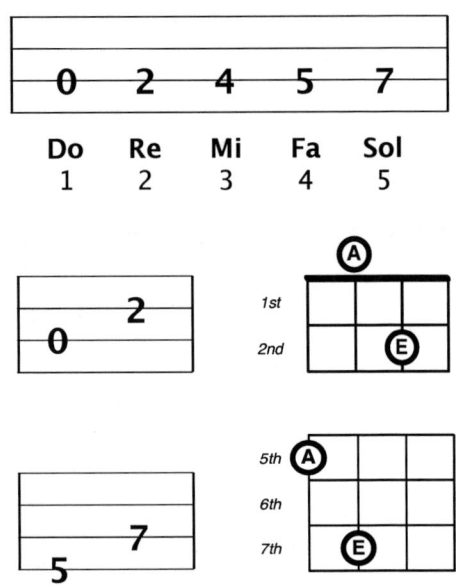

Let's start again down in Open Position. From the open **A** note, move up *5 steps* in the Major Scale: **A - B - C - D - E**. (The **C** is actually C "sharp." Later.)

So that note at the 7th fret of the **A** string is the **E** note and it functions as the **5th degree**. But we can find a unison **E** note 5 frets lower on the **D/2nd** string, at the 2nd fret:

And of course you can take the open string out of it by playing both notes in 5th Position.

More jargon: We call the musical distance between these two notes an **interval** of a **5th**.

Obviously, you would play the **A** note with the 1st finger, but what about the **E** note? Try it with the 3rd finger and then with the 4th. It's more of a reach for the 3rd finger, but it's good to stretch it a little. As for the 4th finger, if it feels tentative, you can always lean your 3rd finger into it: Land with the 4th, support with the 3rd.

Try several **Root-5th** riffs, first in Open, then in 5th Position.
The first one is the Classic Rock Groove plus the note at **Count 4+**:

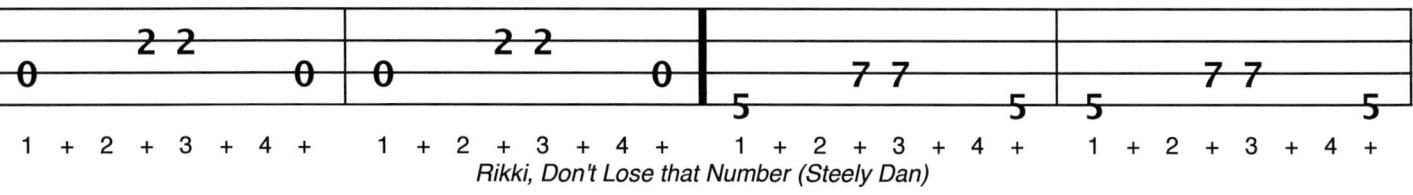

Rikki, Don't Lose that Number (Steely Dan)

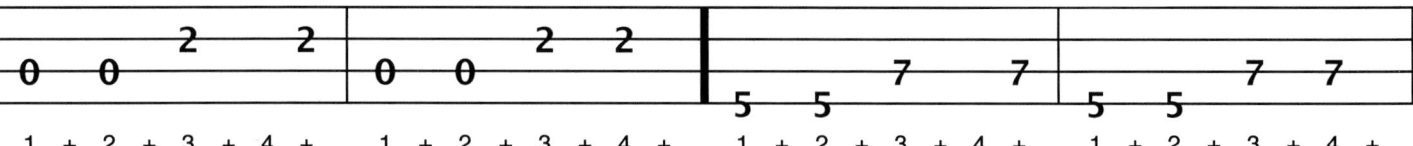

Adding the Low 5th

Frankly, it's just as popular to alternate the **Root** with the **Low 5th**, particularly in country music. What I mean is this: We've established that the **5th** degree of the **A** scale is the **E** note, and we've found two unison locations for it. *But there is another E note that is one octave below the others, **the one on the open 4th string**.*

Well, there are multiple octaves in music. A full size piano has a range of 11 octaves, and a regular 4-string bass has almost 3 octaves. The Musical Alphabet contains 7 letters, **A-B-C-D-E-F-G**, and it starts over with **A** again in the next higher octave, and so on.

The upshot is that there is about *half an octave of notes* below the open **A** note on the **E/4th** string. So let's see what it's like to play **R - Low 5th** in both Open and 5th Positions; of course, there's no other place on the neck to find the low **E**, so we use it both times. (So is this Open Position or 5th Position? The unequivocal answer is, uh, yes!)

This first riff works for just about any country song, then the others get fancier, and you'll need to do some damping:

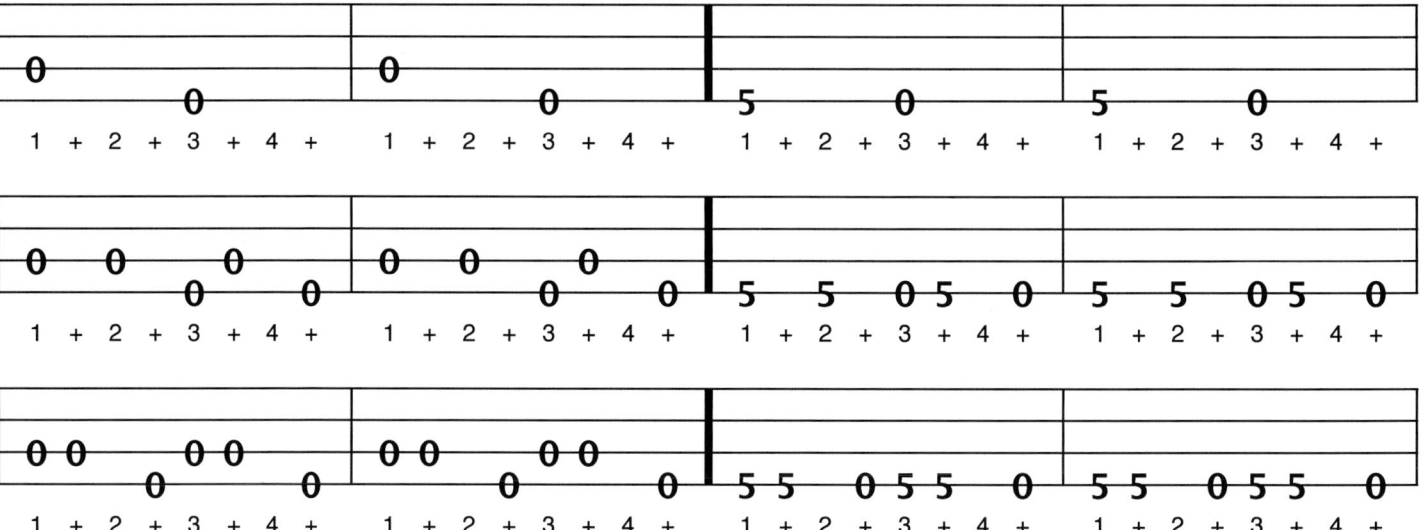

Boy, if you don't damp those open strings, it sounds like therez a-storm a-coming. My left hand wants to deaden just about every note. I much prefer the 5th Position, where my 1st finger alone can control the ringing with a simple release of pressure.

Compare the two approaches using Linda Ronstadt's "Blue Bayou" riff. This one uses both the higher and the lower **5ths**, in a variation on the Classic Rock Groove. (Spoiler alert: Definitely way too boomy in Open Position.)

(Just as the low and high **A** notes are one octave apart, so are the high and low **E** notes.)

I want to mention something about **syncopation**. A syncopated note is one that starts on an "**and**" count and *does not end* right away. The note at **Count 2+** is one such note. It sounds *early*, as if you are rushing, by a half beat, a note that rightfully belongs on **Count 3**. (If you *also* had a note on **Count 3**, it wouldn't sound so weird.)

With that note on **Count 2+**, you *intend* to jump the gun a little, but then you must WAIT all the way until **Count 4** to play the next note. *And I swear:* **Count 2+** *is the* **coolest** *count.*

This one-bar variation on the **CRG** is the first bar of a 2-bar Afro-Cuban rhythm called **Clave** (*clah-vay*); we'll have more to say about that later. Think "Piña Colada Song." I want to call this first bar **Half-Clave**, because this abbreviated version shows up a lot.

Combining the Root, the 5th and the Octave

I know, you'd like to go absolutely crazy, and perhaps run wild, but try to stay **CALM**.

But before exploring a little, there are some extra fingering considerations. *We're going to start to need to move rapidly between fretted notes.* Let's try some *Half-Clave* examples.

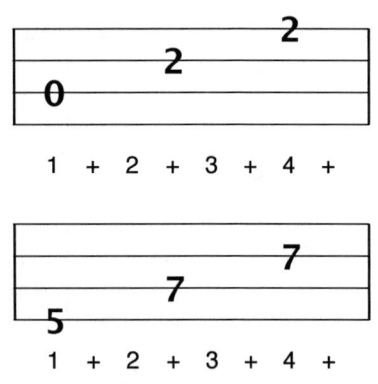

In the Open Position case, I would use a **finger roll** with the 1st finger, where you place the tip of the finger on the first **2**, then roll it or flop it over onto the second **2**. It's not exactly a 1st-finger barre, since you don't want the 2 notes ringing together.

You can do a finger roll in 5th Position, too, with the 3rd or 4th finger (my own 4th finger is *not* a great roller). You could also use the 3rd finger on the first **7** and switch to the 4th finger for the second **7**. Finger numbers:

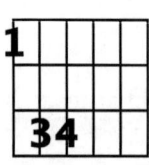

*Fascinating sidebar: If you're a guitar player, you've probably learned about **Power Chords**, which are 2- or 3-note chords composed of either (1) the **Root** and the **5th** or (2) the **Root**, **5th** and **8th**. These chords are Rooted on the 6th and 5th strings, and the 6th-string guys look like this:*

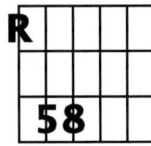

*Since the lower 4 strings on the guitar are tuned **one Octave** above the 4 strings of the bass, the R-5-8 shape is just the same on the bass. Of course, you don't strum bass notes, you play them one at a time.*

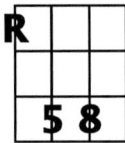

It's amazing how many combinations you can make of 4 notes (**R**, **8th**, **5th**, **5thL**) over the course of 4 or 8 beats of music. Of course, the vast majority of them will *not* sound wonderfully. Here come some of them now, products of my own doodling:

We'll come back to add more scale degrees later, but let's see how the *simpler riffs*, *involving just the **Root***, get deployed when the chords actually dare to *change* on you.....

Chords, Chords, Chords

So a bassist doesn't actually strum chords the way a guitarist would. The frequencies of the strings on a bass are too low for you to strum a 4-note chord without creating total mud. Find a piano and play something like a **C** chord, which would sound GREAT in the middle of the keyboard, but try it down low at the *left* end. What a jarring jumble of jeezly junk. No, you'll need to play *individual notes* out of a chord, most commonly the **Root Note**.

A brief recap: We started this whole mess with a single note, the **A** note, and generated the **A Major Scale**, the 8 notes of the **Do-Re-Mi** song. Then we singled out 3 of the 8 for special consideration, the **Root (R)**, the **Octave (8th)** and the **Fifth (5th)**:

We found some unison positions for these notes and created some riffs using various rhythm patterns, such as the Classic Rock Groove and the Half-Clave patterns.

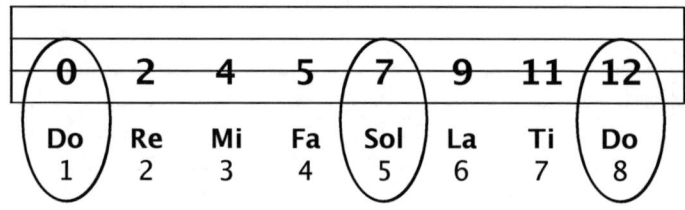

*The one thing we have not yet done is to **change chords**.*

The two **A** notes and the **E** note belong to the **A chord**, but for the moment, we'll ignore the **5th** and **8th,** and focus on the **Root** as the sole representative note for the **A** chord. (We'll bring back those notes soon, and add the **3rd** in a later section to create what is called the **A Triad**, the most basic kind of **A** chord.)

Now this is going to require a shift in your persepective. (Noooo!) Yes. I said before that the **Key of A** includes the **A Major Scale** PLUS the *chords* that *belong* to the **A Major Scale**.

Every one of the 7 different notes in the A Major Scale GIVES RISE to a different chord, and all 7 chords belong to the Key of A. We'll go into more detail later; first let's just see a quick and dirty method for determining *the 3 most important chords in the Key of A*:

Lay out the Musical Alphabet of 7 letters starting with the **A** note and pick off the *1st, 4th and 5th letters*, which turn out to be A, D and E:

A	B	C	D	E	F	G
1	2	3	4	5	6	7

These letters represent the **A chord**, **D chord** and **E chord**, and they are considered to have a **Major Chord Quality**.

Guitarists know them to correspond to the shapes to the right: Bassists just need the three individual *notes*, **A**, **D** and **E**.

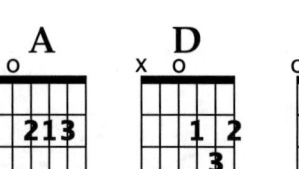

The 1 - 4 - 5 System: Key of A

This is Really BIG. Getting a handle on the **1 - 4 - 5 System** will guide you through all the bass playing you will ever do, and the nice thing is that it's not so complicated that you can't put it directly to use.

I should point out that that there should be some **sharp** symbols (#) in that sequence of chords.....And they're right, but that's for later. It's just not critical for our current porpoises. You don't need to be floundering around just for the halibut.

Again, we'll define a **KEY** as a group of chords that is centered around *one particular chord*, which we call the **1 chord**. In the **Key of A**, also known as the **A Chord Family**, the **A** chord plays a *commanding role* when all these chords get together in a song. The **A** chord exudes what is known as a *Key Feeling* among these chords. It is the Home Chord. It is Restful. When you are playing in the **Key of A**, the **A** chord is usually the first, last and most frequently-played chord. The **4** and the **5 chords** are subsidiary to the **1 chord**, in the way that Spock and McCoy are subsidiary to Kirk.

The rest of the bridge crew play *minor* roles, and I'm trying to be cute here: Most of the other 4 chords in the Chord Family do, in fact, display what is called a **Minor Chord Quality**, the sad sound of the Minor chord in contrast to the happy sound of the **1 - 4 - 5** Major chords. *The **1 chord** is magnetic, the **4 chord** is friendly and the **5 chord** has an expectant, edgy presence (it's known as the Dominant Chord).*

So let's play, for the **Key of A**, the simplest **1 - 4 - 5** chord progression there is. You know where the **A** note is, and from knowing how the bass is tuned, you might further remember that the open 2nd string bears a **D** note and the the open 4th string bears an **E** note, so there are your three **Chordal Root Notes**. (The **Root Note** of the **Key of A** is **A**, but each chord is said to have its own **Root Note** as well.)

Here are the **Root Notes** of the **A, D** and **E** chords in the CRG (gray notes optional):

And here's another way to do it, using the higher octave **E** note on the 2nd string:

Other Keys

*Every key has its own unique set of 1 - 4 - 5 chords, as we collectively refer to them, and there are **thousands** of 1 - 4 - 5 songs in the folk, pop, rock and country genres that contain those three chords exclusively.*

For now, I want you to be able to identify **1 - 4 - 5 chords** in *a handful of Major keys:* ***C, A, G, E,*** and ***D***. This group of keys is usually referred to as, yep, the **CAGED keys**.

Key of E

Let's do the same process with the **Key of E**. Lay out the 7 letters, pick off your **1 - 4 - 5**s:

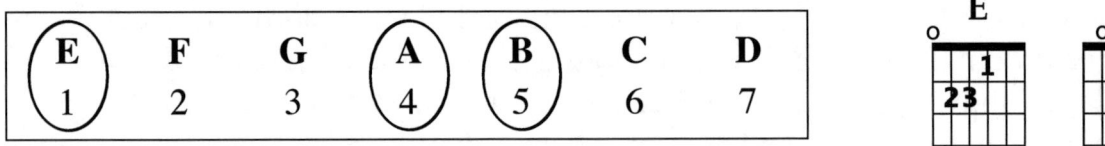

So **E**, **A** and **B** are the **1 - 4 - 5 chords** (though guitarists prefer the **B7** chord). Notice that there is a **two-chord overlap** between our two keys, the **E** and the **A** chords. *Every chord has its own key and appears in two others, acting as a **4 chord** in one and a **5 chord** in the other.*

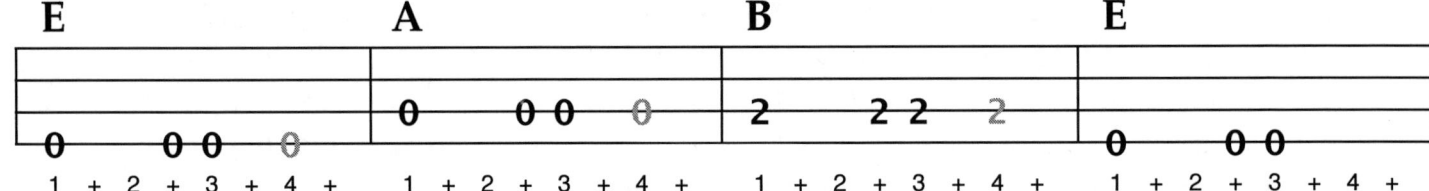

Key of D

Let's do the same process with the **Key of D**. Lay out the 7 letters, pick off your **1 - 4 - 5**s:

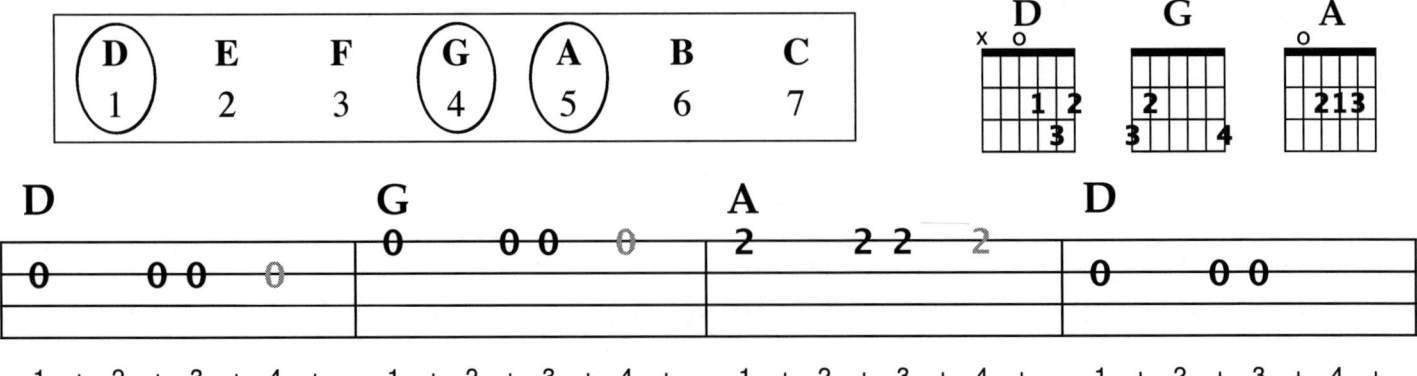

*I started with the **Keys of A, E** and **D** because I knew that their patterns on the neck were similar, only starting on different open strings. The next two keys will require more fretted notes.*

Key of G

Same thing with the **Key of G**. Lay out the 7 letters, pick off your **1 - 4 - 5**s:

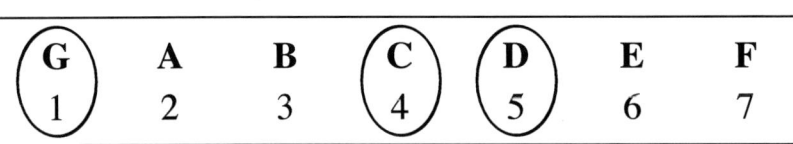

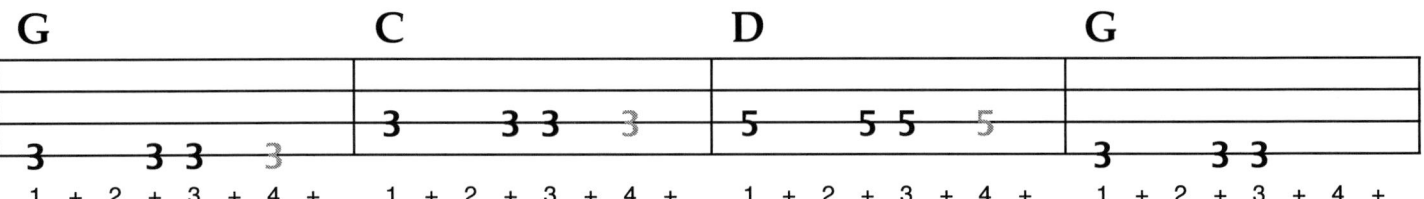

Stop right there*! This is NOT the preferred bass pattern for the **D** chord.*
*Better to take the **unison D** note at the 5th fret of the **A/3rd** string. Try it in 3rd Position:*

Key of C

Same thing with the **Key of C**. Lay out the 7 letters, pick off your **1 - 4 - 5**s:

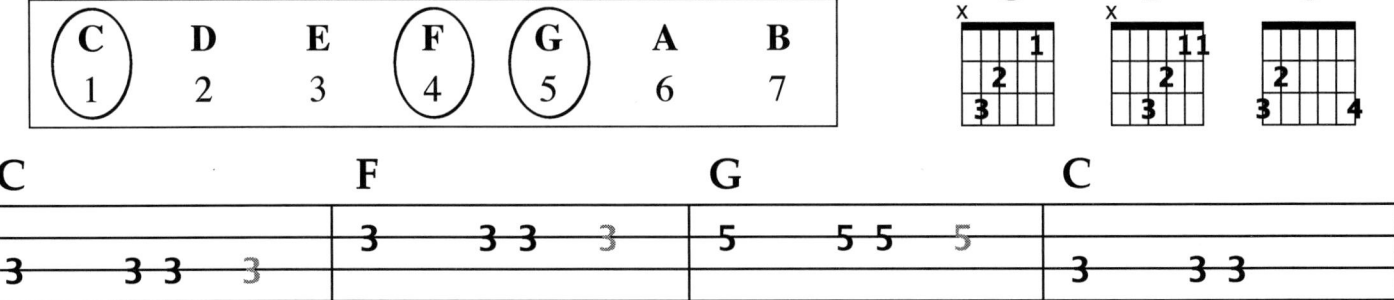

I wonder if you see a *pattern emerging on the fretboard.....*
An "inverted L-shape," perhaps? We're going to call this pattern
the *Universal 1 - 4 - 5 Pattern*. Wherever you go on the neck,
you can use this pattern of Chordal **Root Notes** to play
the 1 - 4 - 5 chords in any of the twelve keys.

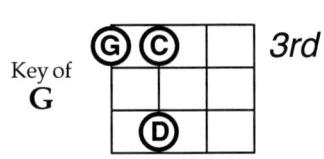

Let's return to the **Keys of A**, **E** and **D** and substitute the fretted
unison notes for all the open-string notes we used a minute ago.....

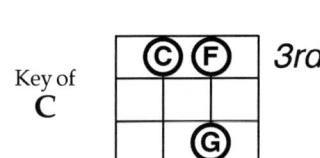

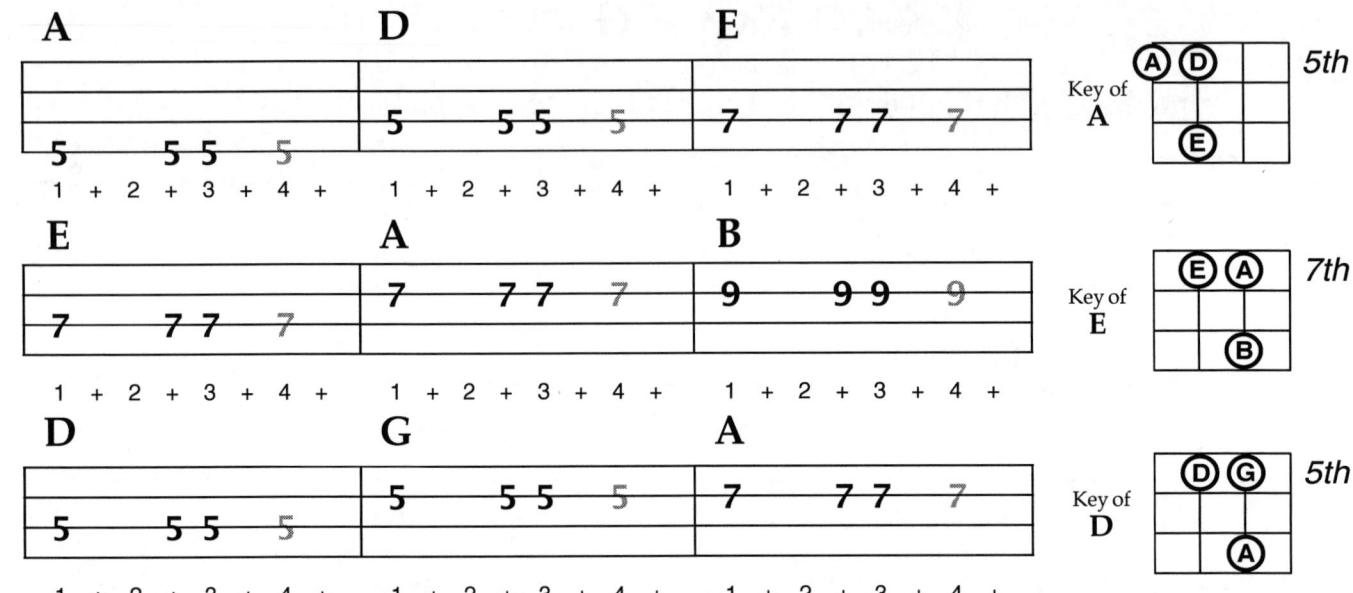

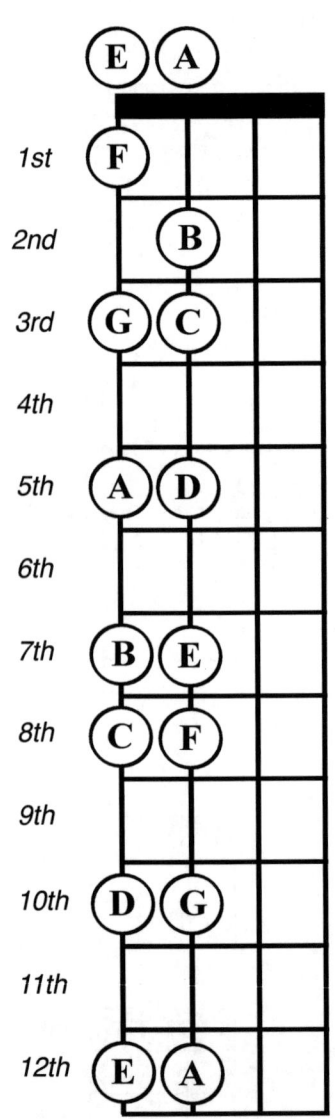

Here's a Fretboard Diagram of all the **natural notes** on the two lowest strings on the bass, the **E/4th** and the **A/3rd**. The natural notes are **ABCDEFG**, but you can see some other unoccupied frets mixed in there, and those notes are called the **accidental** notes. Each one is known by two names: **sharp**, meaning *1 fret higher*, and **flat**, meaning *1 fret lower*.

So the accidental note between **F** and **G** on the 2nd fret of the **E** string can be called either **F-sharp (F#)** or **G-flat (G♭)**.

While the *CAGED keys* are the most popular, you've got these pitiless *guitarists* who will slap a capo on any old fret where they can sing most comfortably, and that will change the key to *who knows what*, but if you poke around a little, you can find the **Root Note** for the key. That's a matter of **ear training**. Or they'll tell you the key, if they know it.

Okay. You need to back up a **1 - 4 - 5** song in the **Key of B**. You can park the **1 chord** from the Universal Pattern either on the **A/3rd** string at the 2nd fret or the **E/4th** string at the 7th fret. That will give you **B - E - F#** as the **1 - 4 - 5 chords**. Duck soup!

Need the **Key of E♭**? Park it at the 6th fret of the **A/3rd** string, which will produce the **1 - 4 - 5 chords** of **E♭ - A♭ - B♭**. Done!

You don't really need to know the *names* of the **4** and **5 chords**. Just park your **1 chord** and ride the Inverted-L train! Beauty!

By now, you've learned enough from this book to do competent 1 - 4 - 5 backup for any key they might throw at you. Ain't life grand? All you'd need is a song sheet with the guitar or piano chords (same thing) placed over the words and one of our (or *your* own) grooves.

*About this **ear training** thing*.....With time and experience, your ear will more easily pick out the **Root Note** for any song that you will be expected to accompany. Heck, there are only 12 different possibilities, right? Remember, the **1 chord** will most likely be the first, last and most common. Then just listen to the guitar or keyboard (or symphony orchestra) for the ***strongest*** note, usually the one that is lowest in pitch. Your percentages will improve over time. I find that, when comparing notes, the higher strings (in pitch) on the bass are the easier for me to hear, so I track down the note on the **G** or **D** strings and then drop down the octave (go down 2 frets and 2 strings) to identify it.

*Meanwhile, **read the rest of this book**!* You'll (1) get more practice hearing and playing the ***1 - 4 - 5 chords***, as well as the other chords in the Chord Family, (2) learn how to add more notes from the Major Scale and (3) start using the Pentatonic Minor (Blues) Scale.

1 - 4 - 5 Examples

Well, now that you *can* play **1 - 4 - 5**s in all 12 keys, let's *not* (and say we did).
What I mean is that, since the layout of the **1 - 4 - 5**s is the same all over the neck,
if you learn something in one key and position, it works for (most of) the others.

Okay, here's a basic **1 - 4 - 5 - 1** pattern using various grooves, some old, some new.
Let's put these in the **Key of D** in 5th Position (3rd pattern down, top of the previous page).
In the **Key of D**, the **1 - 4 - 5 chords** translate to **D - G - A**:

D   **G**   **A**   **D**

Shift the note at **Count 4** a half beat later. **Counts 1** to **2** are symmetrical to **Counts 3** to **4**:

Half-Clave:

22

Shift the note at **Count 4** a half beat later. Makes it sound funkier:

```
|-----------------|-----------------|-----------------|-----------------|
|                 |  5   5     5    |  7   7     7    |                 |
| 5   5     5     |                 |                 |  5   5          |
|-----------------|-----------------|-----------------|-----------------|
 1 + 2 + 3 + 4 +   1 + 2 + 3 + 4 +   1 + 2 + 3 + 4 +   1 + 2 + 3 + 4 +
```

Delete the 3rd note altogether. That's about as sparse as you'd generally want to get:

```
|-----------------|-----------------|-----------------|-----------------|
|                 |  5   5          |  7   7          |                 |
| 5   5           |                 |                 |  5   5          |
|-----------------|-----------------|-----------------|-----------------|
 1 + 2 + 3 + 4 +   1 + 2 + 3 + 4 +   1 + 2 + 3 + 4 +   1 + 2 + 3 + 4 +
```

Let's do a *meager* **1 - 4 - 5** song survey to see what's running around out In The Wild.
You'll get to play the same basic shape in different keys on different parts of the neck.
In most of these examples, the chord changes come twice as often (every half bar).
For now, don't worry about the letter names of the chords, just play and listen.

In the first three, the chord sequence is **1 - 4 - 5 - 4**, with a return to the **4** ahead of the next **1**.
The first riff is in the **Key of F**. Early on, you play Half-notes, and later on, Eighth-notes:

```
 1        4         5        4         1         4          5          4
|-----------------|-----------------|-----------------|-----------------|
|                 |                 |                 |                 |
|     1           |  3       1      |           1 1 1 | 3 3 3 3 1 1 1 1 |
| 1               |                 |  1 1 1 1        |                 |
|-----------------|-----------------|-----------------|-----------------|
 1 + 2 + 3 + 4 +   1 + 2 + 3 + 4 +   1 + 2 + 3 + 4 +   1 + 2 + 3 + 4 +
                   Don't Come Around Here No More (Tom Petty)
```

This one is in our old friend, the **Key of A**. It's all Quarter-notes except for a delay on **Count 3**:

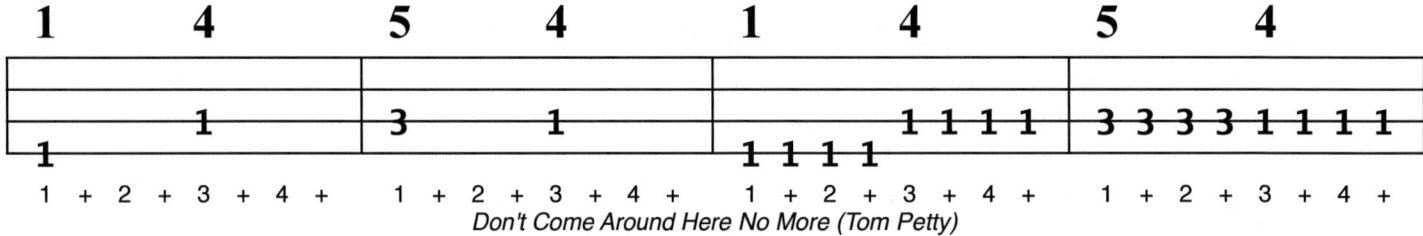

Wild Thing (The Troggs)

The third riff is in the **Key of D**, but I want to build it up gradually, from no syncopation
to the Real Thing. Same sequence, four versions, with a new note displaced each time:

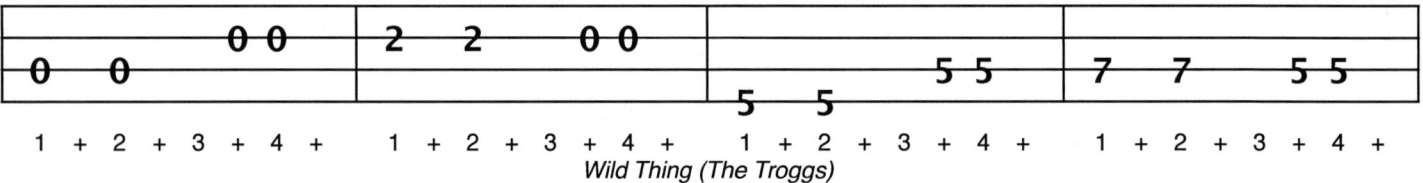

Good Lovin' (Young Rascals)

Here's one with the **4 and 5 chords** flipped around: **1 - 5 - 4**. Interestingly, it has the same rhythmic pattern as the first bar of the previous riff: same syncopation, but now **Key of C**:

```
  3   3   5   5 3   | empty measure |   3   3   5 5 5 3 | empty measure
1 + 2 + 3 + 4 +     1 + 2 + 3 + 4 +    1 + 2 + 3 + 4 +   1 + 2 + 3 + 4 +
```
Let My Love Open the Door (Pete Townsend)

(Technically, on these last two, the chord change happens at the syncopated note on **Count 4+**.)

But so many rock and roll songs are completely overrun by plain ole Steady Eighth Notes, with no syncopation. "Every Breath You Take," "Brass in Pocket," "Still R&R to Me," the list goes on and on. Here's an obscure example, though it did reach #2 on the Billboard 100 in 1981. The **1 - 4 - 5**s are all jumbled up here; it starts on the **5 chord** and roams around in the **Key of D.** This is a good spot to focus on the strict alternation of the pick (Down-Up) or fingers (Up-Up).

```
  5           4              1                    5           1            4
7 7 7 7 5 5 5 | 0 0 0 0 0 0 0 0 | 7 7 7 7 0 0 0 0 | 5 5 5 5 5 5 5 5
              | 5 5 5 5 5 5 5 5 |         5 5 5 5 |
                play one or the other
1 + 2 + 3 + 4 + 1 + 2 + 3 + 4 + 1 + 2 + 3 + 4 + 1 + 2 + 3 + 4 +

  4           5              1                    4           5            1
5 5 5 5 7 7 7 7 | 0 0 0 0 0 0 0 0 | 5 5 5 5 7 7 7 7 | 0 0 0 0 0 0 0 0
                | 5 5 5 5 5 5 5 5 |                 | 5 5 5 5 5 5 5 5
1 + 2 + 3 + 4 + 1 + 2 + 3 + 4 + 1 + 2 + 3 + 4 + 1 + 2 + 3 + 4 +
```
Queen of Hearts (Juice Newton, yes, JUICE Newton.....my friend Heather went to high school with her.....)

As long as we're cheating on Fave, the Inverted-L, with that open string, this is pretty neat:

*You can play the **Root Notes** of the **1 - 4 - 5 chords** all on the SAME FRET if you go for the **Root** of the **5 chord** that is BELOW the **Root** of the **1 chord**. Same fret, lower string.*

We saw this before when we were talking about the Major Scale and looking for the Lower **5th degree**, remember? Now, you need to KEEP THIS **STRAIGHT**:

*The **5th degree** represents a **note** in a **scale**, but the **5 chord** is a **chord** in a **chord family**. A whole different thang. Same notes on the neck, but different **functions** for the bassist.*

So here comes an example in the **Key of B**, with a **1 - 4 - 1 - 5** sequence and the CRG:

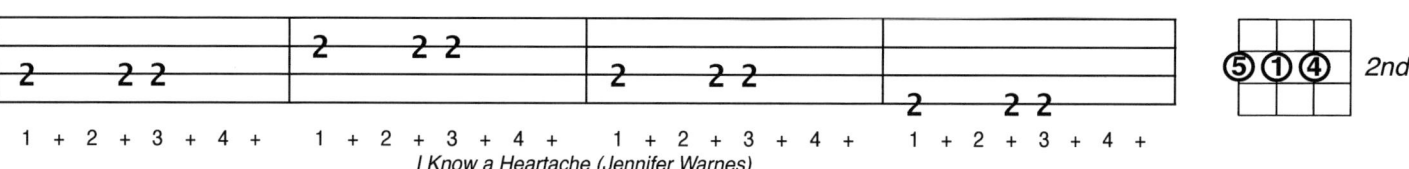

I Know a Heartache (Jennifer Warnes)

The 5 Chord versus the 5th Degree

I don't want to let this issue go just yet, because in the section on **Triads**, it gets even trickier. See, the **5th degree** of the Major Scale has two functions:

(1) as just another note in a scale, albeit the second most important note in the scale, and (2) as a Chordal **Root Note** that *gives rise* to the **5 chord** in the Chord Family.

It's the same note on the neck of the bass, but (confusingly) in the first case it represents *a note within a chord*, and in the second case it represents *a chord within a chord family*.

We'll use an example in the **Key of D**, although, as you know by now, it truly matters *not* which key we use, because they all work the same way.

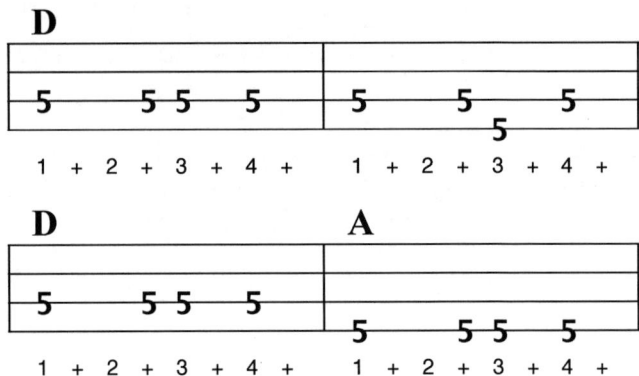

This is 2 bars of the CRG over the **D** chord, where the 1st bar contains all **D Root Notes** and the 2nd bar shows a single alternation to the lower **A** note, the **Low 5th degree**.

But THIS is one bar of **D** chord containing all **D Root Notes**, followed by one bar of **A**, a *Low 5 chord*, containing all **A Root Notes**.

I hope I'm not whomping you over the head too brutally with this, but you do need to see the distinction now, before you get too tangled up in notes and chords.

Now, how do we *know* that that second bar is a change to the **Low 5 chord** and not just an extended, 4-count alternation to the lower **5th degree**? This is going to sound evasive, but *we just know*. The experienced musical ear says, "Yeah, no, if you *don't* mean to change the chord there, I need to hear more **D Root Notes** to feel.....musically stable. Comfortable." If it's *supposed* to be a chord change, then the rest of the band must change as well, please.

So How Much Is Too Much?

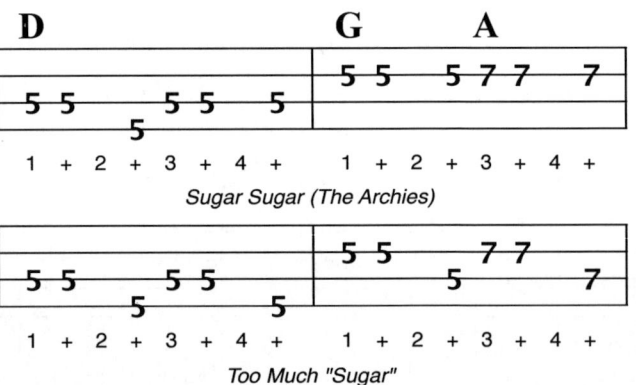

Here's a **1 - 4 - 5** passage in the **Key of D**. The top version has one alternation to the **Low 5th** in the **D** chord while the bottom version has it *4 times* over all 3 chords.

I think Jughead got it right: Once was enough. Once was fine over the longer stretch of **D** chord, but too messy over the faster **G** to **A** changes. (You'll decide for yourself as you go along.)

Sugar Sugar (The Archies)

Too Much "Sugar"

How About a Lower 4 Chord?

It's hard to resist pulling on a thread. Now that you know about the **Low 5 chord**, it's only a step away (literally a step *down*) to find the location for a **Low 4 chord**.

Now we have an "L" shape hooked onto our "Inverted-L."
I think the diagram to the right is pretty self-explanatory.
Notice that from the "0 fret" you can reach the **Roots** for
the **1 chord**, a **High 4 chord** and a **Low 5 chord**. Then
it's down 2 frets for a **Lo 4** and up 2 frets for a **Hi 5**.

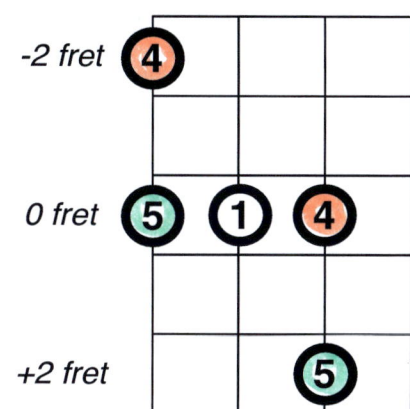

Clearly, this principle won't apply to a **Root Note** on the
E/4th string, since there IS no lower string to find notes on,
but you could adapt it to **Root Notes** on the **D/2nd** string and
recreate the rest of the pattern there. Now, in the **Key of D**:

1	Hi 4	Hi 5	Hi 4	1	Lo 4	Lo 5	Lo 4
	5 5 5 5	7 7 7 7 5 5 5 5					
5 5 5 5				5 5 5 5			
					3 3 3 3	5 5 5 5 3 3 3 3	

Let's revisit the "Queen of Hearts," starting with the **Lo 5 to 4** and ending with **Hi 4 to 5**:

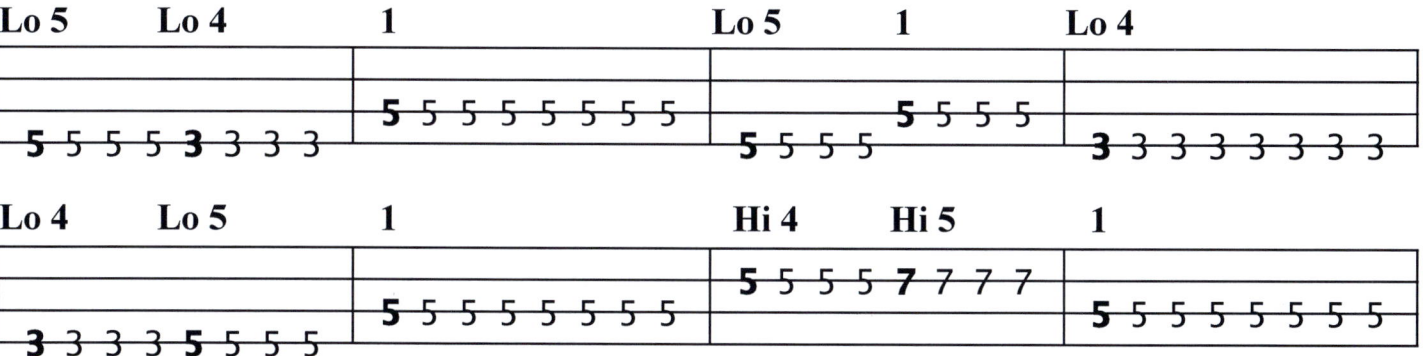

Time to combine! We're going to sneak the ***5th degree*** back into the picture. We'll have the country **Root-5th** structure, with both **High** and **Low 5ths**, for all three of our **1 - 4 - 5 chords**.

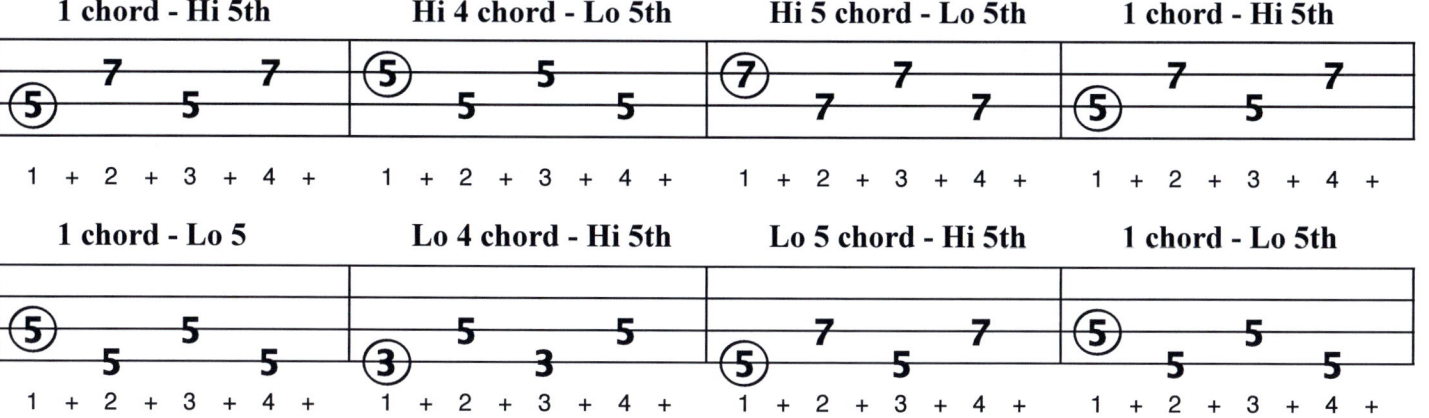

Triads

I hope you can see that we keep bouncing back and forth between *two main themes*:

(1) Using the Major Scale to enhance a bass part *within a chord*. So far we've incorporated the **Root**, **High 5th**, **Low 5th** and **Octave** (really only 2 different notes and their octaves).

(2) Moving *from chord to chord* within a key. So far we have used only the **1 - 4 - 5 chords**.

Time to bounce back to the *scale*: We will add one more note from the Major Scale, **the 3rd**, in order to create **the Triad**, *which is composed of the* **Root**, **3rd** *and* **5th** *of any Major Scale.*

For a breath of fresh air, let's take the **Key of C** and the **C Major Scale** for the example. Again, it doesn't matter *what* key we use, because all this stuff works for all 12 keys.

Here are Tab diagrams of the first 5 degrees of the **C Major Scale**, first going straight up the neck from the **C Root Note** on the **A** string, and then shifting to the **D** string and proceeding up that way, hitting unison versions of the same notes. Play them both:

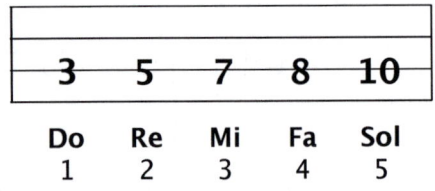 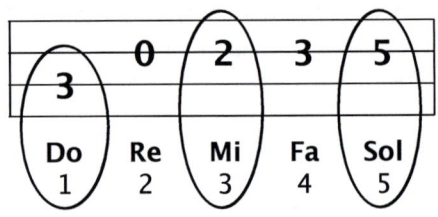

Well, the second approach is the more useful one because we can reach all three notes in what is called the **C Major Triad**, as well as the **Octave**, without needing to shift the left hand very much.

So we play the notes of the **C Triad** ("Major" is implied) here in 2nd Position, meaning that the 1st finger is in charge of the 2nd fret. But this means that the *2nd finger is assigned to the **Root Note*** at the 3rd fret. Then the 1st finger plays the **3rd**, and the 3rd or 4th finger plays the **5th** and the **8th**.

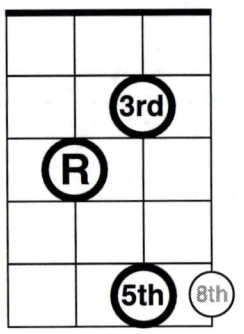

But that's not the end of the story! Because you know that most notes on the bass can lay claim to a **unison version** located *5 frets higher* on the neck on the *next lower string* (in pitch).

So we can move the shape of the **C Triad** to the **E** and **A** strings in 7th Position, with the same finger assignments. Any advantage to playing in 7th Position over 2nd Position? Well, the frets are closer together higher on the neck, so it's less of a stretch, and you'll see other differences soon.

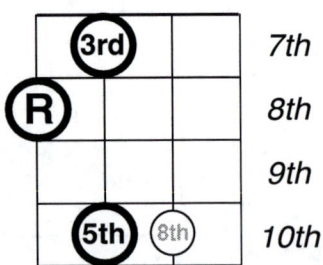

1 - 4 - 5 Examples with 1 - 3 - 5 Triads

See what I mean about it getting messier? Well, this is as bad as it gets. It's so easy to bandy about the terms "**1 - 4 - 5**" and "**1 - 3 - 5**," and people get them mixed up right and left. Look at it this way:

*Each chord member of the **1 - 4 - 5** is constructed FROM its own **1 - 3 - 5**; that is, from its own Chordal **Root Note** plus the 3rd plus the 5th.*

The **1 - 4 - 5** operates at the chord level, while the **1 - 3 - 5** exists at the note level (the notes that are nested within chords). We'll look at all the details of this later, including naming all the notes in the scale and seeing how to build the triads, but you know enough now to get cracking on practical application.

Okay, back to this Universal Triad Shape. It takes up two adjacent strings, and the **Root** is found on the lower of the two strings. So you can play this structure on *only three pairs of strings*, the **E/A**, **A/D** and **D/G** pairs:

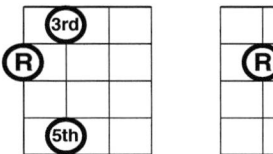
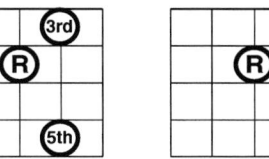

Put your 2nd finger on the **Root Note** for the chord you are being asked to accompany (check the diagram to the left), and you'll be in prime position to *u-n-l-e-a-s-h* the Triad. Below are 4 scenarios for playing simple Triads over the **1 - 4 - 5 chords** on different pairs of strings with **Roots** at the 5th fret. Don't worry about the actual chords, just the numbers. The first two have **Hi 4/5 chords** and the second two have **Lo 4/5 chords**:

28 Oh yeah, there's another scenario, where the three Chordal Roots are all at the same fret, where the **1 chord** is rooted on the **A/3rd** string and there's a **Hi 4 chord** and a **Lo 5 chord**:

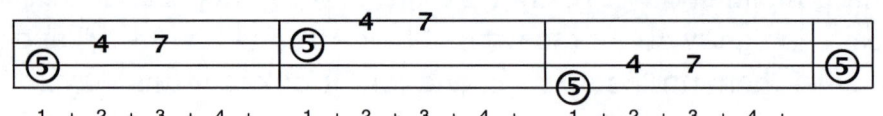

I know this seems like a lot to keep track of, but essentially, it's just two bits of information:

(1) Where are the **Roots** of the **1 - 4 - 5 chords**? Your 2nd finger is in charge of those.....

(2) And then, where are the **3rds** and the **5ths** in relation to those Chordal **Roots**?

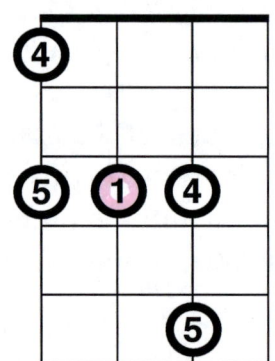
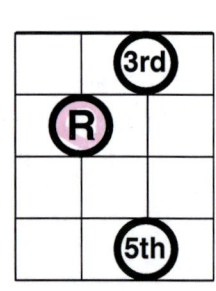

Here are some **1 - 4 - 5** riffs in a variety of keys that make various uses of the Triad. I'll give you (1) the letter name of each chord and (2) its number in the chord family.

This first one in the **Key of G** is about as square and straightforward as can be:

G / 1   C / 4   D / 5

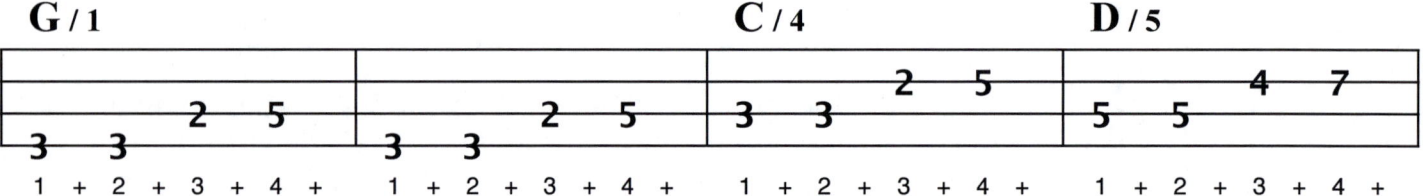

Now a Half-Clave riff in the **Key of C** played over what we call a **Twelve Bar Blues** progression:

C / 1

F / 4   C

G / 5   C

Hound Dog (Elvis Presley)

Here's another one in the **Key of C** that's a little more active for the left hand:

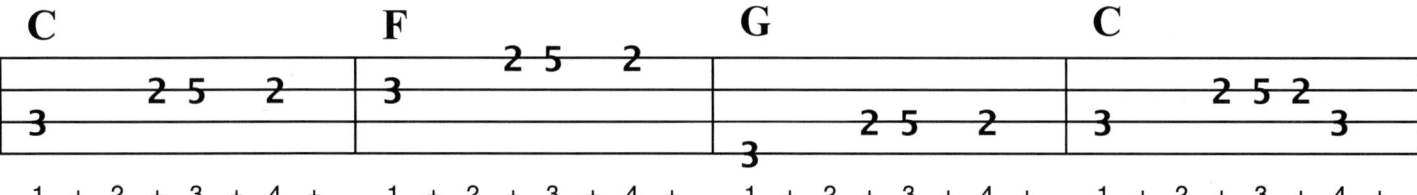

Delay the 2nd note by a half beat to get a CRG, and go **Lo 5 chord** to stay in 3rd Position:

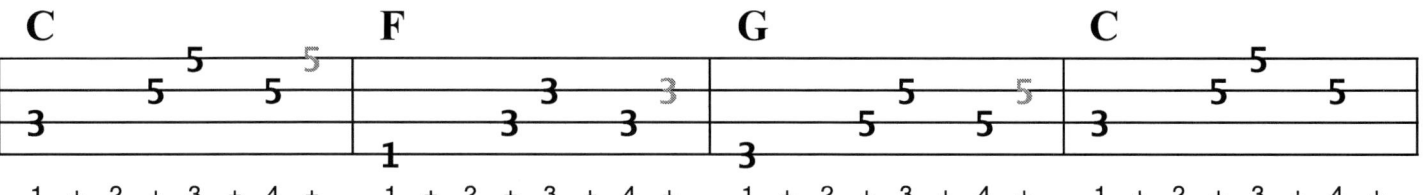

Now go **Lo 4** and **Lo 5** and add a another **5th** at **Count 4+**. Notice the open **3rd** in the **F** chord:

[tab: C | F | G | C with patterns 2 5 2 5 / 0 3 0 3 / 2 5 2 5 / 5 2]

Just for the sake of comparison, the next riff has the same rhythm as the one above, but it includes the **8th** instead of the **3rd**. Notice how it sounds stronger without the **3rd**, but drier:

[tab: C | F | G | C with 5s and 3s]

Remember to either: (1) use the finger roll between the **5th** and **8th**, or (2) switch from 3rd to 4th fingers. In any case, you don't want those notes ringing into each other.....Mute!

We've really put the pressure on the left hand now to keep moving, but also to stay on each note for its full duration, whether a Quarter-note or an Eighth-note. Hang on Sloopy, hang on! *Paradoxically, the only way to get a smooth sound from your bass is to stay on each note for as long as you can, and then **bolt** for the next note as fast as you can. **Sonic continuity**. But don't let any of those notes overlap, either, or you'll wallow in the mud.*

Here are a couple riffs where the chord change is syncopated half a beat early:

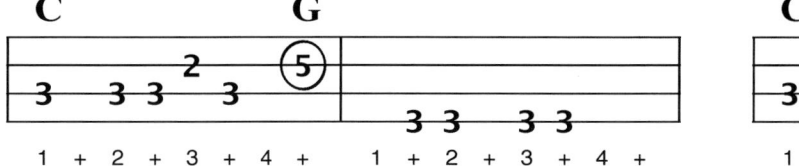

Let's do one more page of Triad stuff, try a few different keys, different techniques. These first three all have syncopated chord changes. We've had syncopated notes before, but this is the first time they will appear *right at the point of a chord change.*

This first one is a textbook case, where you can really compare a syncopated note with its unsyncopated predecessor in a straight **1- 4 - 5** context. **Key of B**, half-clave in the 3rd bar:

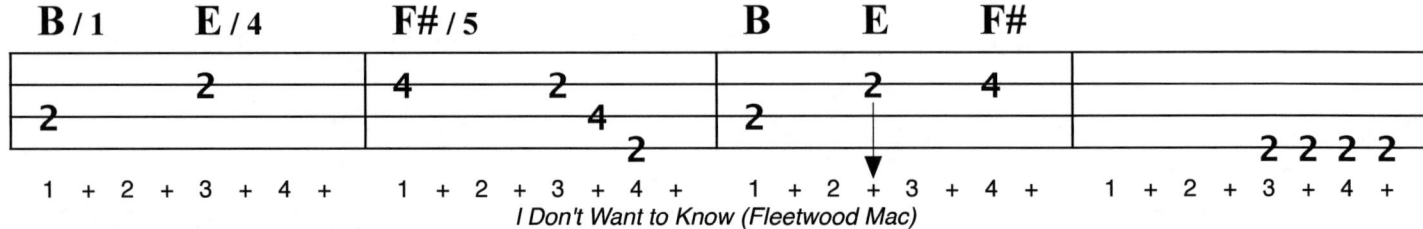
I Don't Want to Know (Fleetwood Mac)

Here's an active little **1 - 5 - 4 - 5** riff in the **Key of D** with 4 chord-change syncopations:

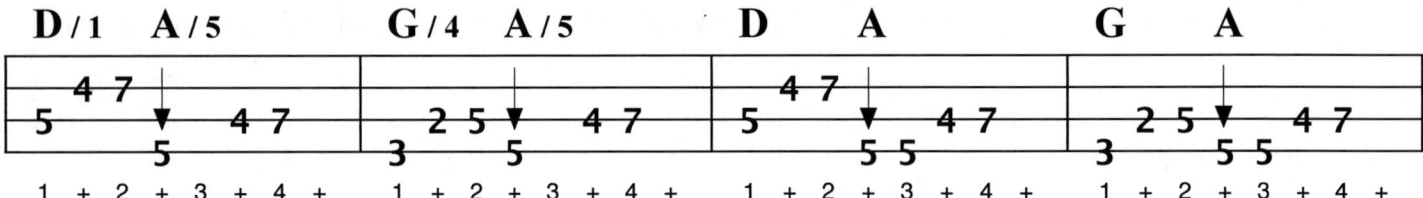

The next one, back in the **Key of C**, is a bit trickier. That first arrow shows a syncopation that is ***not*** at a chord change. The riff starts with a **C Root**, but the arrow note is an ***E note***, which is the 3rd of the C Triad. Yes, **3rds** can exist below **Roots** as well as **4ths** and **5ths**. The second arrow *does* point to a syncopated chord change:

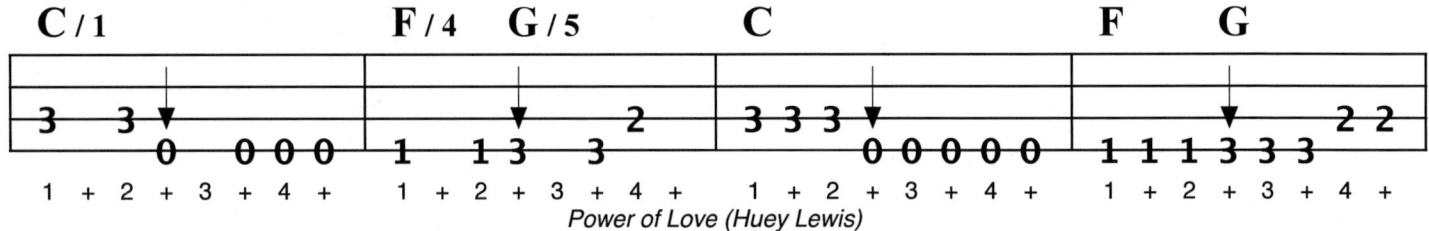
Power of Love (Huey Lewis)

You can also find a higher **unison 3rd** that is on the same string as the **Root**, because, as you are by now *so* well aware, you can find a unison note for most notes on the bass by moving to a lower string (in pitch) and going up 5 frets. But why would you ***want*** to, since it's a 4-fret jump from the **Root**? Well, what if you wanted to **Slide** into that **3rd**?

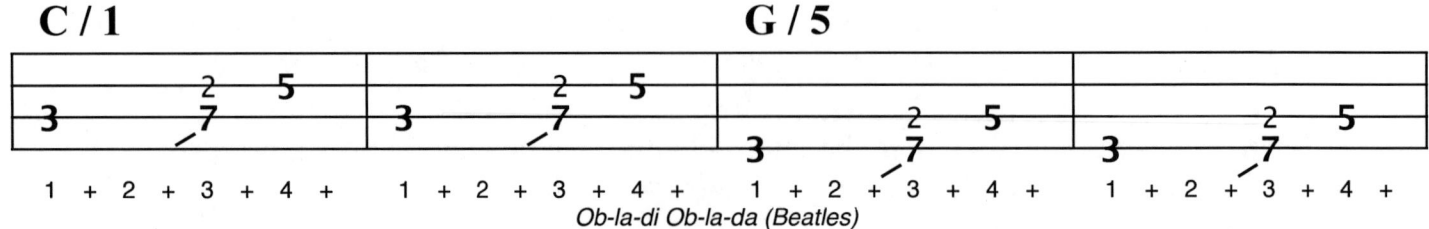
Ob-la-di Ob-la-da (Beatles)

Play the **Root** at the 3rd fret, then land with your 4th finger at, maybe, the 5th fret and ***quickly*** slide up the string while continuing to press down on it until you reach the 7th fret. You slid.

Several thoughts before we move on:

(1) If the **Root** of the Major Scale is on the **E/4th** string, then the Chordal **Roots** for the **4** and **5 chords** will be *higher*, on the **A/3rd** string. You can do Triads, requiring 2 strings, and Octaves, requiring 3 strings for the **1, 4** and **5** chords.

(2) If the **Root** is on the **A/3rd** string, the Chordal **Roots** may be *higher* or *lower*, on the **D/2nd** string or the **E/4th** string. And you can do the 2-string Triads and the 3-string Octaves in all positions. *This is the sweet spot.*

(3) If the **Root** is on the **D/2nd** string, then the Chordal Roots will be *lower*, on the **A/3rd** string. You can do Triads and Octaves on the **4** and **5 chords**, but only the *Triad* works for the **1 chord**, since the Octave needs an extra string, which you don't have. *But* you'll find the same **Root Note** *one octave lower* on the **E/4th** string by moving down 2 frets and down 2 strings (in pitch).

So you have the most playing options if the **Root** of the Major Scale is on the **A/3rd** string. You can play Triads and Octaves both high and low on all the chords for the **Keys of B, C, D** and **E** (plus the accidentals). For the successive **Keys of F, G** and **A**, this is getting a bit high on the neck. You might be better off dropping down the octave to find the **Roots** on the **E/4th** string.

The Value of the 3rd in the Triad

You know, the **Root Note** of the Triad is the Boss, the Head Man, Top Dog, Big Cheese, the Head Honcho. The **5th** is Number Two, the Spiro Agnew, the John Oates, the Second in Command that helps with the structure of the chord. Together, the **Root** and **5th** represent the foundation and framing of a house. The **3rd** is more how you decorate the house and make it a home. It's softer, rounder and warmer than the other two.

I like the *Star Trek* analogy, which I used for the **1 - 4 - 5** situation with the Chord Family, but I think it works at the **1 - 3 - 5** level as well. The **3rd** is the emotional one, the changeable one with the ups and the downs, the Leonard "Bones" McCoy. In the Major Triad, the interval between the **Root** and **3rd** is known as a **Major 3rd**, which gives the Triad its happy outlook. Without it, you're left with the **Root** and the **5th**, also known as a **Power Chord**, and that sort of says it all. It has a strong but hollow sound. The **3rd** gets us to join hands and sing, *"All You Need Is Love."* (More about the *Minor* 3rd later.)

Very soon now, we'll be looking to play all the degrees in the Major Scale, but I want to spotlight *one more note* beyond those in the Triad: the **6th**. Then we'll be able to have a bit of fun playing boogie-woogie, boy. You know, the bugle one from Company B.

Adding the 6th: Boogie-Woogie

Boogie-woogie is a distinctive dance-oriented piano style that seems to have been developed by African-Americans in the Piney Woods of northeast Texas in the 1870s. Little known fact. And you'll recognize it when you hear it. Have a listen to some of these songs on YouTube: *"In the Mood"* (Glenn Miller); *"Jailhouse Rock"* and *"Blue Suede Shoes"* (Elvis); *"Lucille"* and *"Good Golly Miss Molly"* (Little Richard); *"Great Balls of Fire"* and *"Whole Lotta Shakin' Goin' On"* (Jerry Lee Lewis) and *"Barbara Ann"* (Beach Boys).

We start on the open **A/3rd** string and lay out the Major Scale up to the **6th** (left). But the more useful version of the scale stays in Open Position, switching over to the **D/3rd** string, affording us a nicely symmetrical pattern of notes:

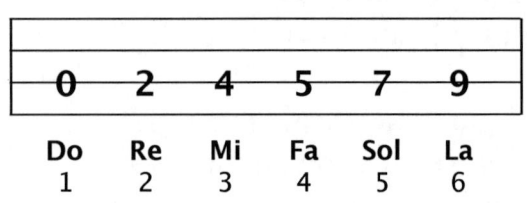 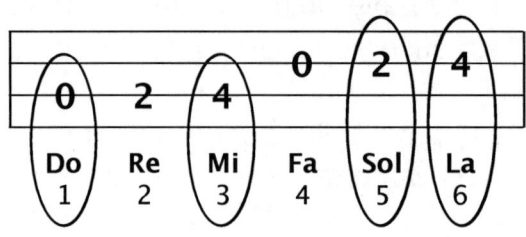 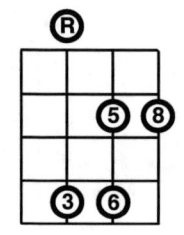

For the boogie pattern, start with the Triad, add the **6th**, go to the **8th** and c'mon back:

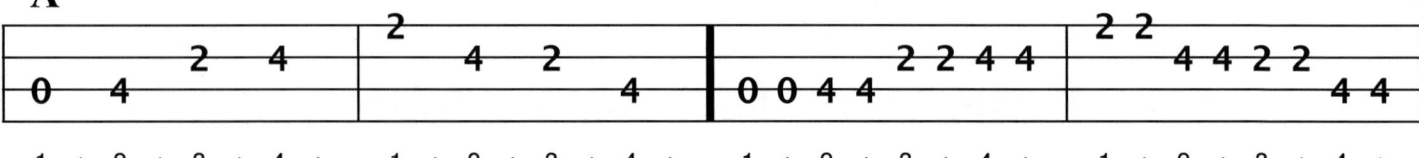

Any of you youngsters remember the Andrews Sisters from the 1940s? They did *"Boogie Woogie Bugle Boy of Company B,"* but more to the point, they also recorded *"Beat Me, Daddy, Eight to the Bar."* It's not what it sounds like; it's the rhythm pattern in the above 3rd and 4th bars, where you play those eight Eighth-notes per bar.

Typically, the chord progression is the **Twelve Bar Blues** progression that you first saw when we introduced the Triad, but the boogie pattern goes a step farther, to the **6th**. We won't go the whole nine yards yet, because I mainly just want to introduce the **6th**. There will be a chapter later that spells it out, moving between the **1** and **4 chords** several times, then on to the **5 chord** for a big finish.

But here's a simple 1-bar boogie riff that moves from the **1 chord** to the **4 chord** and back:

```
    A              D      2   4    A                        
                          0   4                  2   4            2   4
        2   4                              2   4          
    0   4                                  0   4            0   4

1 + 2 + 3 + 4 +   1 + 2 + 3 + 4 +    1 + 2 + 3 + 4 +   1 + 2 + 3 + 4 +
```

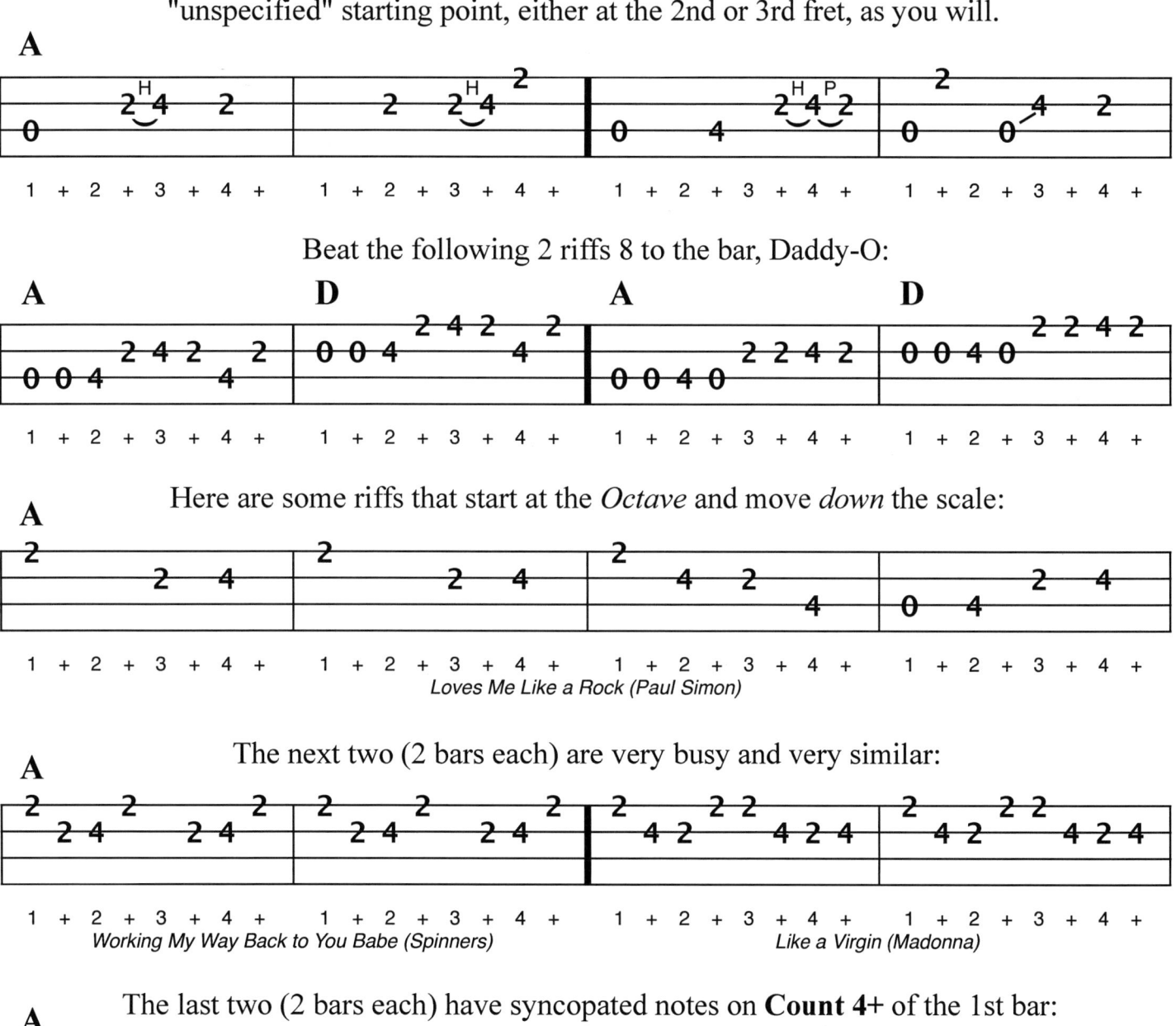

The Major Scale, At Last

I've been dangling this thing in front of your face for some time now, holding back on you, but really, it was for your own good. If I had started you off with this stuff, you might have fled like a striped baboon. Now, you have some practical experience with notes, frets, strings and chords, and what I'm about to impart to you won't seem so distressingly alien. Believe me, if I can understand this stuff, you can get it, too.

I want to approach this material absolutely *from scratch*, as if you didn't already know some bits and pieces of music theory. This way, I won't leave out anything, and it's good for the brain to run through the same information from a fresh angle.

Okay, so there are 12 musical notes. (Still with me?) It helps to think of them as being laid out in a sequence, from left to right, where each successive note is a little higher in **pitch** than the one before it. Think of the piano keyboard:

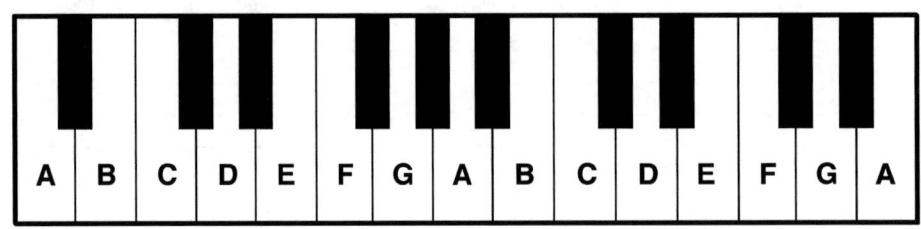

But things get a little annoying right away, because there are only 7 different letters of the alphabet (**A - B - C - D - E - F - G**) that are employed to name the 12 notes, so lemme see, that's.....5 notes left over that still need to be named.

The 7 notes are called **natural** notes. Those other 5 are called **accidental** notes, and each one of them can be assigned either a **sharp** name or a **flat** name. For example, **A** and **B** are natural notes, but there is *another* note that lies between them, and you can call it **A-sharp (A#)**, meaning that it's one note *higher* than the **A** note, *OR* you can call it **B-flat (B♭)**, one note *lower* than the **B** note. And there are 4 more notes like this. Oh yeah, these are the black notes on the piano keyboard.

The reason to have both flat and sharp names may *eventually* matter to you, but that's all you need to know right now. *To keep it simple, we'll just use the **sharp** names for the notes.* So here's the layout of the 12 notes in music, the 7 natural and the 5 accidental notes:

A - A# - B - C - C# - D - D# - E - F - F# - G - G#

The scholars among you will notice that there is no accidental between **B** and **C**, nor between **E** and **F**. *This is one of the few things in music that you need to know cold.*

The C Major Scale

Why start with the **C Major Scale**? It doesn't even have a **Root Note** on an open string!

It seems that the **Key of C** has been favored above all other keys to have *no accidentals*. If you know the piano keyboard, you know that you can play all the white keys (ivories) from **C** to **C** and produce a perfect **Do - Re - Mi** Major Scale. Let's take a look:

This is the best picture of a Major Scale you'll ever see. The white keys are the natural notes, and the accidentals, the black keys, are situated *exactly* where the Whole-steps *skip over* in the **Key of C**. You know the "2 Wholes" and the "3 Wholes"? All the black keys are in those (w)holes.

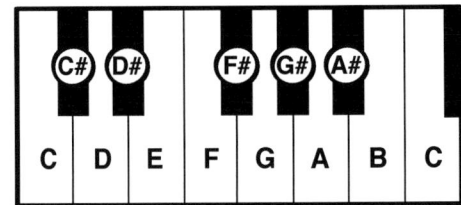

Let's lay out the **C Chromatic Scale** and pick off the Whole- and Half-steps:

(C) - C# - (D) - D# - (E) - (F) - F# - (G) - G# - (A) - A# - (B) - (C)

Whole   Whole   Half   Whole   Whole   Whole   Half

Yup, it works. We hit only natural notes. *But this will happen **only** in the **Key of C**, starting on the C note. Starting on **any other note** will bring in at least one accidental.*

There is a **C** note at the 3rd fret of the **A** string. Let's start there and do Wholes and Halves:

C Major Scale

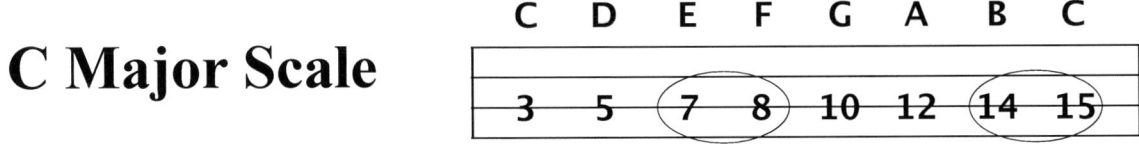

I like the optics here: You can SEE the single-fret, Half-step intervals between **E** and **F** and between **B** and **C**, and the 2-fret Whole-steps everywhere else.

But in practice, this is no way to play a scale, there's too much traveling. Let's stay down the neck and find *unison notes* so we can stay *in position*:

```
        C   D   E   F   G   A   B   C
                                2   4   5
                        2   3   5
                3   5
```

This sequence of notes is called the **Chromatic Scale**. "Scale" comes from *scala*, Latin for "ladder." When you reach the top of the ladder, you start over again with **A**.

Really, the Chromatic Scale is no more than a listing of all the available notes there are, and it's *not* the most important scale in music. THAT honor belongs to the **Major Scale**. The Major Scale is the Big Kahuna, the scale from which most other scales can be derived. *But we need the Chromatic Scale, the Raw Material of Music, to generate the Major Scale.*

Technically, there are 12 different Chromatic Scales, each one starting on a different note and including all 12 notes. So the **A Chromatic Scale** starts and ends on **A** and includes all the notes. Likewise, the **B Chromatic Scale** starts and ends on **B** and includes all the notes. Seems a bit silly, except that we'll derive each Major Scale from its own Chromatic Scale.

Each Major Scale contains 7 notes out of the 12, and no two Major Scales contain exactly the same set of notes, although most scales overlap to a degree.

And there is a procedure for deriving these scales. But first let's establish a measure of *musical distance* between two notes, known as an **interval**. Let's define the **Half-step** and the **Whole-step**:

A **Half-step** is the distance between 2 consecutive notes in the Chromatic Scale, a difference of 1 fret on the bass, say from **A** to **A#**. It's our smallest interval.

A **Whole-step** is equal to two Half-steps, a difference of 2 frets on the bass, say from **A**, skipping over **A#**, to **B**. This is the more common interval.

Now we can apply a formula to any Chromatic Scale to derive the *infinitely* more useful Major Scale. ***Here it is, the Golden Rule, the absolute foundation of Western music:***

Start on the first note of any Chromatic Scale, which is the **Root Note**, and travel:

2 Whole-steps, then **1 Half**-step, then **3 Whole**-steps, then **1 Half**-step.
Also known as *2 Wholes and a Half, 3 Wholes and a Half.*

The resulting array of notes is called a **Major Scale**, and completes one **octave**, including the 7 notes plus the next higher **Root Note** (*octo* is Vulcan for "8").

Our objective from here on will be to generate Major Scales from the Chromatic Scales, then Chord Families from the Major Scales. ***As a bassist, this is all you will need to know.***

Really, all we've been doing thus far in the book has been
simply filling in the Major Scale with additional scale degrees:

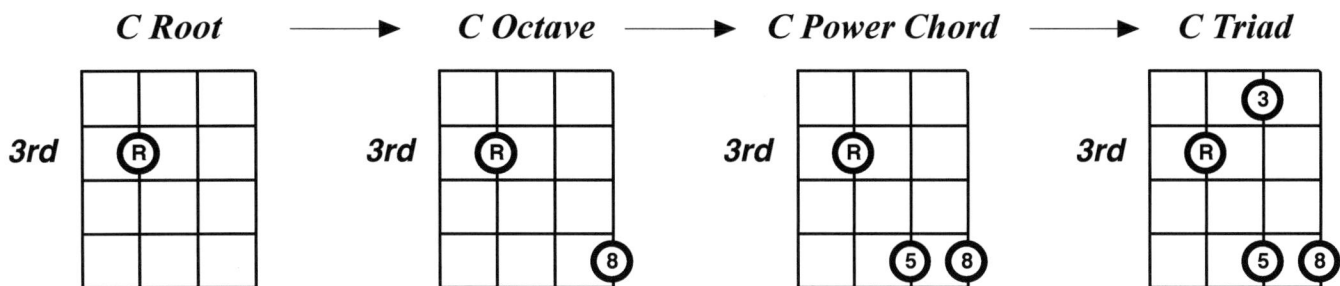

C Major Scale

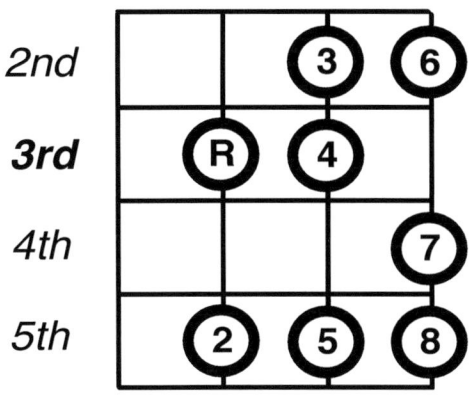

Now we have the Full Monty.

How are you supposed to play this scale? **OFPF**. That is, One Finger Per Fret. The **1st finger** plays the notes on the 2nd fret, **2nd finger** gets the 3rd, **3rd finger** on the 4th and **4th finger** on the 5th.

If you expect to play scales a lot, you'll want to be sure to plant your left thumb near the center of the neck so you can arch your wrist and be able to bring all 4 fingers straight down onto the notes. It's a stretch, but *run the scale up and down.*

But you know that there are *unison notes* for all these: "down" one string and up 5 frets. So there must also be a **C Major Scale** in *7th position* with an **E/4th**-string **Root Note** *having exactly the same shape on the neck:*

This is known as the Universal Major Scale shape.

Find the **Root Note** for *any scale* you need on either the 3rd or 4th string, affix your 2nd finger, and go!

Technically, this **C Major Scale** is in *7th Position*, just as the one above occupies 2nd Position. True that. But as a guitarist, it's my habit to think of this scale as being *at the 8th fret,* since that's where the **Root** lies, and the guitar chord that accompanies this shape has a 1st-finger barre that lies across the 8th fret. Whichever viewpoint suits your fancy.

C Major Scale

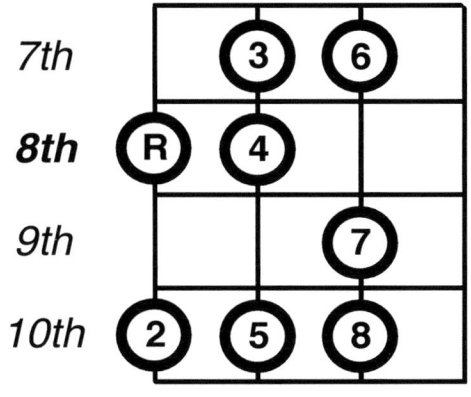

Again, an advantage of playing up the neck is that the frets are closer together so that you don't have to stretch as much, and this is even *more* significant when playing **OFPF**.

C Major Scale in Open Position

I would be sadly remiss if I didn't show you the notes of the **C major Scale** in Open Position. Sometimes these locations come in handy, as you saw in the riff for "The Power of Love" (that low **3rd**).

You get 5 notes of the **C Major Scale** *above* the **C Root Note** and another 5 notes *below*.

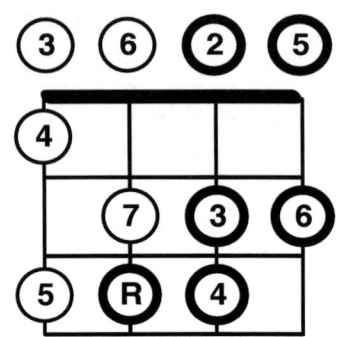

Other Major Scales

Since the **Universal Major Scale** shape is *universal*, there's not much more to say. But I would like to show you how the other **C-A-G-E-D** keys are constructed and discuss some practical considerations in deploying them around the neck.

G Major Scale

Let's start our adventure by picking off the **G Major Scale** from the **G Chromatic Scale**. Apply the *Golden Rule* starting on the **G** Root Note: *2 Wholes & a Half, 3 Wholes & a Half.*

(G) - G# - (A) - A# - (B) - (C) - C# - (D) - D# - (E) - F - (F#) - (G)
Whole · Whole · Half · Whole · Whole · Whole · Half
G A B C D E F#
1 2 3 4 5 6 7

See, when you start on a **G** note, the pattern of Whole- and Half-steps picks up one sharp, **F#**.

There are 2 positions up the neck for the **G Major Scale** (and one down in Open Position). Unlike the **C Major Scale**, *the second one is found **an octave higher**.* The higher octave for **C Major** is *w-a-y* up the neck, and even the higher octave for **G Major** may be a bit too high.

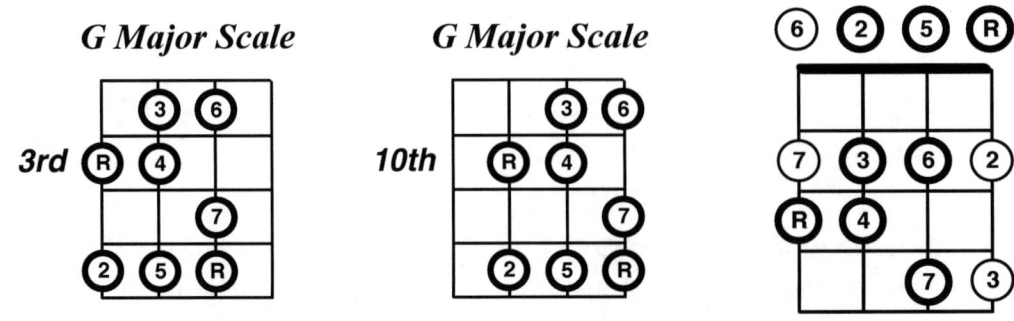

D Major Scale

Start with the **D Chromatic Scale** and apply the Golden Rule:

(D) - D# - (E) - F - (F#) - (G) - G# - (A) - A# - (B) - C - (C#) - (D)

Whole   Whole   Half   Whole   Whole   Whole   Half

D	E	F#	G	A	B	C#
1	2	3	4	5	6	7

This time, the Golden Rule yields 2 sharps, **F#** again and now **C#**.

There are two positions up the neck for the **D Major Scale**, the one we've been using, with the **Root** on the 5th fret of the **A/3rd** string, as well as a *unison* position farther up. But the first one is the most useful, and you should know about the *open* one as well.

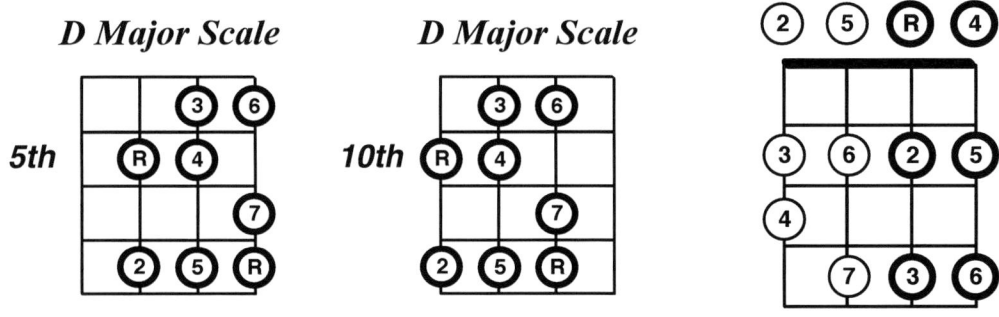

A Major Scale

(A) - A# - (B) - C - (C#) - (D) - D# - (E) - F - (F#) - G - (G#) - (A)

Whole   Whole   Half   Whole   Whole   Whole   Half

This time, the Golden Rule yields 3 sharps, **F#** and **C#** again and now **G#**. I dare say there's a pattern developing here. I chose to talk about the different major scales in this particular sequence of keys (**C - G - D - A**) for a reason:

Key of C has 0 sharps. Go up *5 letters* to determine the next key: **C - D - E - F - G**.
Key of G has 1 sharp, **F#**. Go up *5 letters* for the next key: **G - A - B - C - D**.
Key of D has 2 sharps, **F#, C#**. Go up *5 letters* for the next key: **D - E - F# - G - A**.
Key of A has 3 sharps, **F#, C#, G#**. I'd call that a pretty significant pattern.....

So every time we go up a **FIFTH**, that next key contains whatever sharps were there before and adds one new sharp, and BTW, the sharps themselves are a **FIFTH** apart.

If you are *fascinated* by this revelation, and must know more, let me direct you to my book, **Music Principles for the Skeptical Guitarist, Volume One: The Big Picture**. Everything in there applies to the bass as well as the guitar. What this is all leading up to is a discussion of the **Circle of Fifths**, which is the basis for much of the progressing of chords in music. (Instead of going into that discussion in this book, we will soon go straight to the punchline for some useful tools.)

But let's finish up with the **A Major Scale** and do one more......

The **Key of A** was the first key we worked with, and we just looked at the Open Position for the boogie-woogie style of bassline, so you're pretty familiar.

What's the next key? Count up **5 letters** to find **E**. (And it will have 4 sharps: F#, C#, G#, D#.)

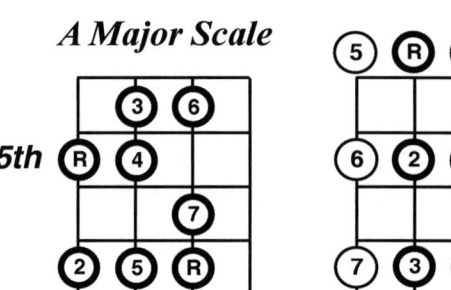

E Major Scale

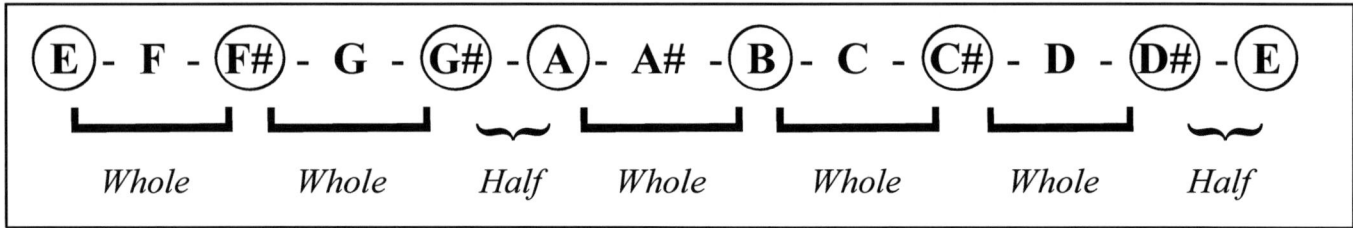

The first position up the neck is the main one; the second one is marginal. But the Open Position will see some use when we return to the boogie-woogie.

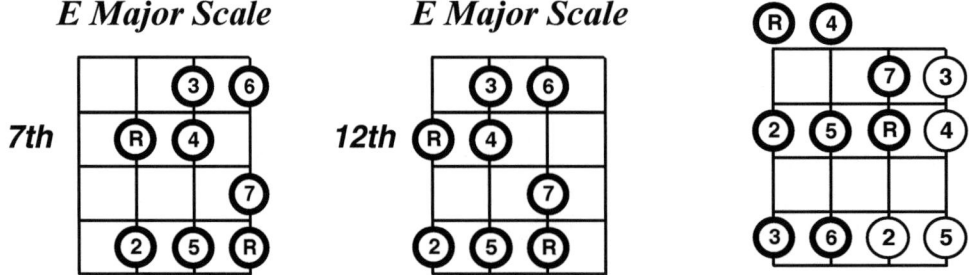

Of course, you'll always be able to find some intermediate note locations that are in unison and can be used to tie together, say, the open and the mid-neck positions. *But generally it's better to work within a position than to chase around between them.*

The Purpose of Major Scales in Basslines

You've come a long way, mio babbino caro. You started out with just the **Root Notes**. Then came the **Octave**, the **5th**, the **3rd**, the **6th,** and now we'll flip all the cards over and allow ourselves to enjoy the rest of the Major Scale: the **2nd**, **4th** and **7th**.

The main use and function of these notes is to connect Root Notes from chord to chord.

Often we like to hear a "walking" effect between chords. And know that you can get by with Less. When you add More, you risk adding Too Much. So exercise caution. It's important that **at least 50% of the notes** you play in a bassline come from the **1 - 3 - 5** of the chord you are accompanying. No less! Otherwise, it's not the chord you think it is.

*That's the thing about the **2nd**, **4th**, **7th** and even the **6th** degrees:* ***They don't harmonize with the mother chord.*** *You can sprinkle them in to provide connection, interest and flavor, but you cannot* ***dwell*** *on them. It is the **1 - 3 - 5 Chord Tones** that hold Music together.*

And yet these Non-chord Tones are critical to Music, since it's *their very dissonance* that propels a song through its chord changes. A little discomfort can be a good thing. A little judiciously applied prod with a pointed stick can work wonders. Without these irritants around, Music just sits there, gaping at the telly, eating chocolate bon-bons.

This dissonance is probably more important to a lead instrument playing the melody, and sometimes the bass itself is called upon to do melodic duty. But mostly, bassists are supporting someone *else* playing the melody, and should try to avoid a "dissing" contest.

So how can we most carefully and effectively fit these Non-chord Tones into a bassline? *We use them as Passing Tones / Leading Tones / Approach Notes*, as they are variously called. I'll circle the Passing Tones in the following examples on a **D** chord:

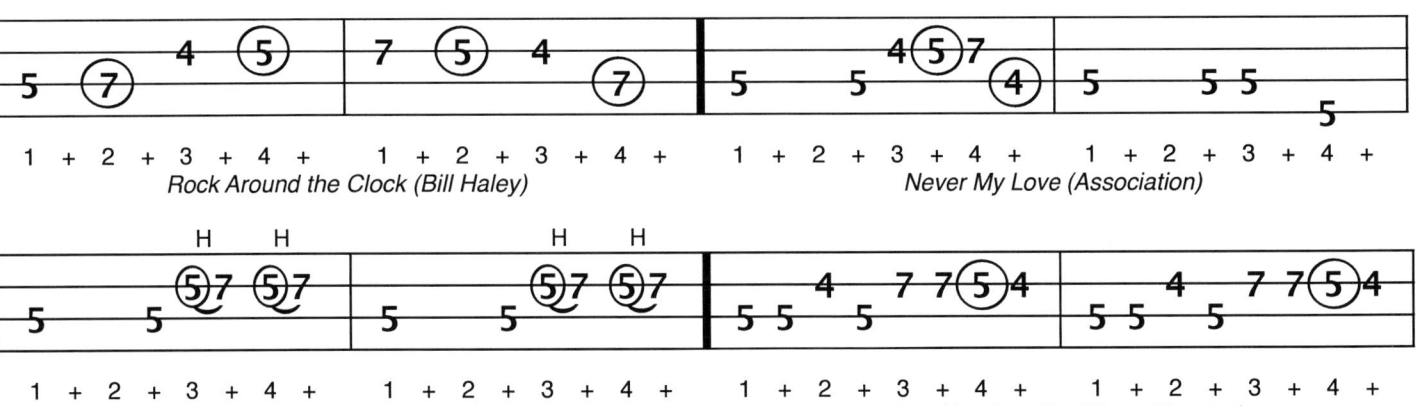

Mostly, these Passing Tones consist of bits of the Major Scale that fill in the gaps between Chord Tones, but sometimes they approach the "target" note from out of the blue, as does the **4** in "Never My Love" and the **5-7** in "Dock of the Bay".

42

Try to be aware of these Passing Tones, but don't stress over distinguishing between the numbers of the scale degrees as you go along. Just try to stay inside the Major Scale and get used to hearing the walking / leading / approaching dynamic that is occurring. DO be a Do-Bee and keep track of which notes are the Chord Tones. That's important.

Actually, we WILL run into some **chromatic** Passing Tones that DO fall outside the Major Scale; you know, those other 5 notes that are interspersed between the 7.

There's another issue that complicates keeping all these notes straight:
Within a key, one chord's Passing Tone will be another chord's Chord Tone!
As we begin to change chords within the Chord Family (as we're about to do) the distinction becomes moot. For example, in the **Key of C**, the **1 chord**, which is the **C** chord, contains the notes **C**, **E** and **G**. So since the **F** note is not one of those three, it would be a Passing Tone. Fine. But when you inevitably switch to the **4 chord**, which is the **F** chord, the notes are **F**, **A** and **C**. So here, the **F** note is a *Chord Tone*, not Passing! And the **C** note is a Chord Tone in both chords!

So go easy on yourself. You *must know* the **Root**, you really *should know* the rest of the Triad (all the Chord Tones), and just be *aware* of when you're playing Passing Tones.

Examples of Passing Tones in the 1 - 4 - 5s

Here are 4 basslines in the **Key of E**, from the **1** to the **4 chord**. Start and end on the **Root**:

E / 1   A / 4

I think some of those sound pretty good, and many of the bars are interchangeable.
Now, staying with the **Key of E**, let's embellish and connect some **1** and **5** chords:

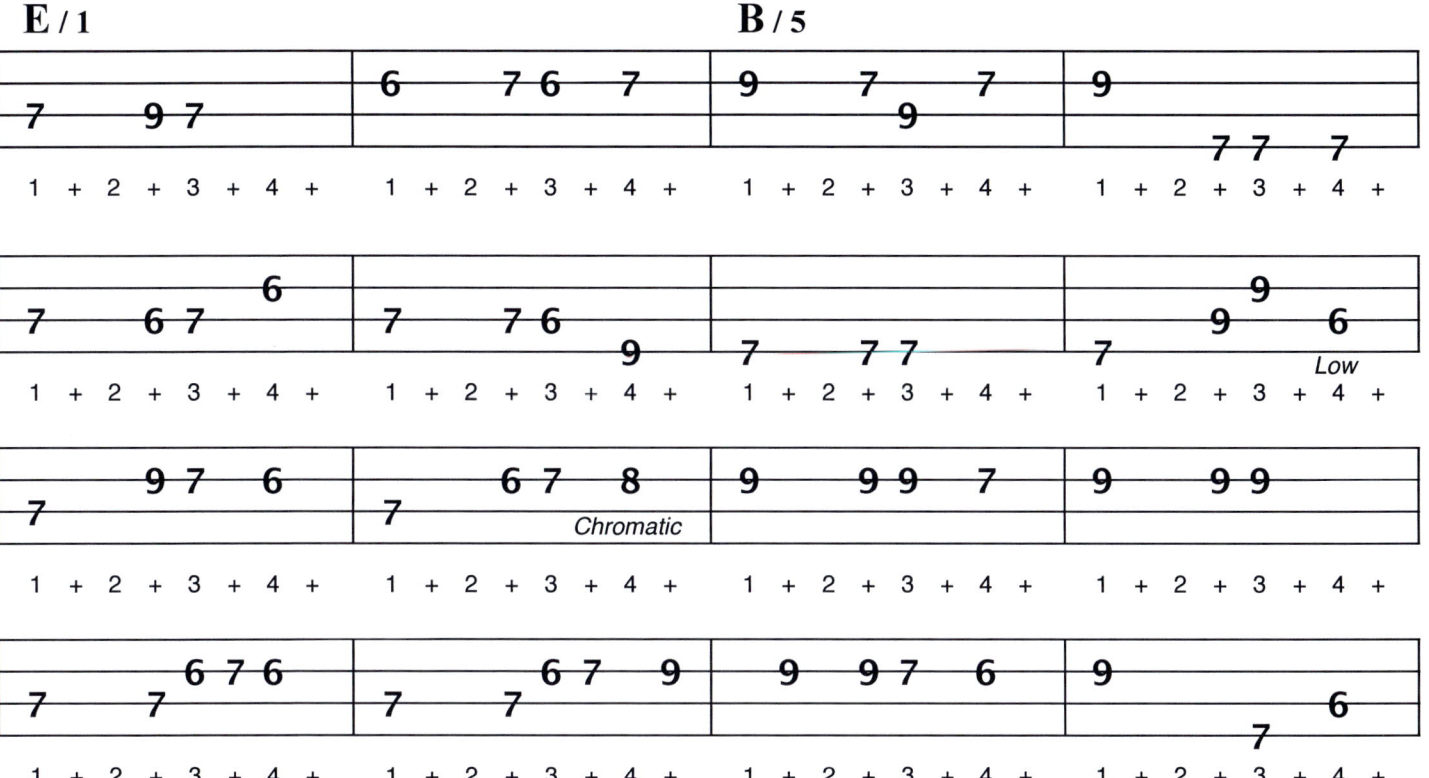

Now let's focus and expand on what could be called the **CCG, the Classic Country Groove**.
Something like it dominates Johnny Cash's "I Walk the Line." This may be the most
straightforward way to connect the **Root Notes** of the **1 - 4 - 5** chords.
Here it is, first in Open Position then in 2nd Position:

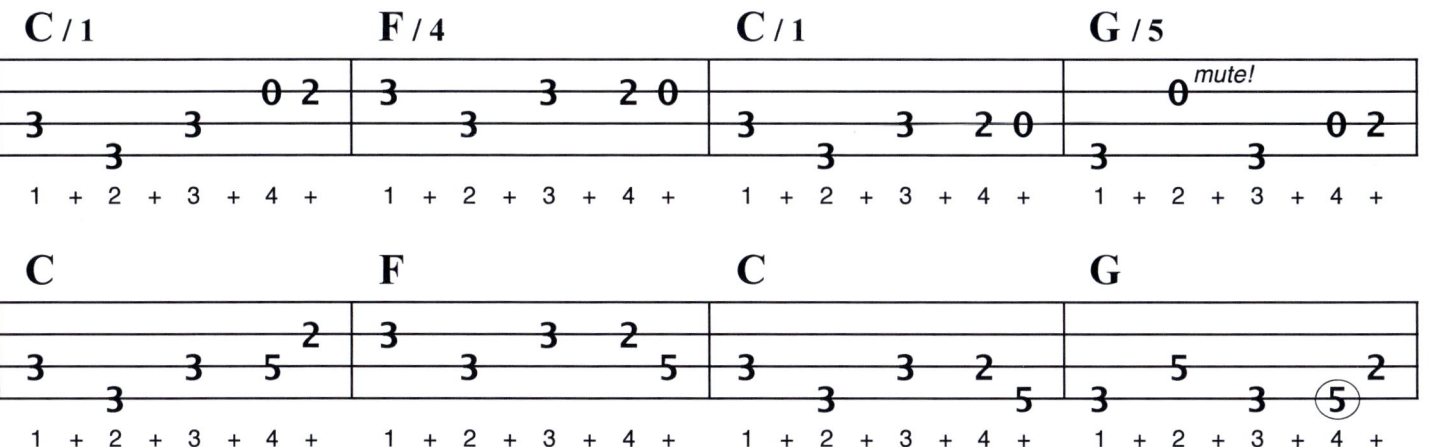

Clearly, the Open Position is easier to get around in with all those friendly open notes.
Gotta work harder to reach all those **5**s that are substituted for the **0**s. But if you play
this passage in just about any other key, you'll need the "all-fretted" approach
(which, as you know, is easier higher on the neck where the frets are closer).

Same chord progression, same **Key of C**, but let's add a chromatic run and a **Hi 5 chord**:

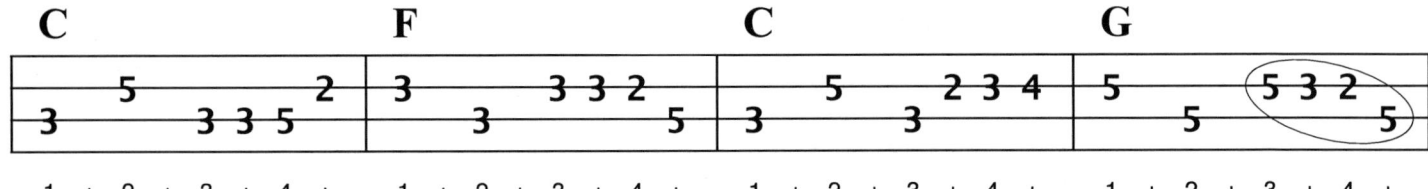

We went to the higher **G** note, then dropped down the octave via the **5th** to the lower **G** note.

To figure out a chromatic run, you usually check how much time you have and how many notes you need to squeeze in. Then you work *backwards* to find the starting note that will get you to the target note on track. Now we keep the whole thing on the *middle two strings*, which means that you need to switch to the **Hi 5th** for **C** and keep the **Lo 5th** for **F** and **G**:

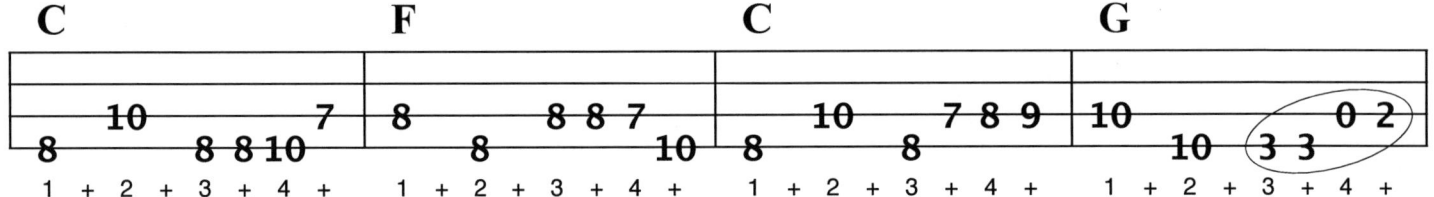

Let's see, what else can we do to this thing? Well, we can toss it up the neck to the *unison* locations for these notes, where the frets are closer together. Of course, the lower notes on the **E/4th** string are not compatible with playing in 7th Position, so there's your trade-off:

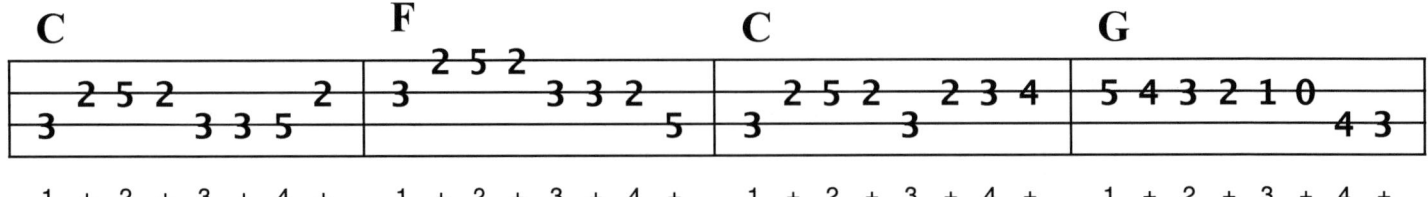

Woh! Unexpected, that little detour back Down the Neck. Maybe the two positions **aren't** so incompatible. I mean, if you decide at the spur of the moment to try something like that, why not? *You can connect any of our positions in any way you like*, as long as you can get there *in time* while ensuring a smooth transition. If it doesn't work, don't do it again.

Let's try this. Let's inject a little more zip with Triads, plus a chromatic run at the end:

C	F	C	G

```
     2 5 2                2 5 2                  2 5 2     2 3 4    5 4 3 2 1 0
3            3 3 5    3          3 3 2     3             3                    4 3
                                       5
```

Well, that was *awful*. I mean, those frenetic Triads are just annoying. And technically, something *like* a long chromatic run might be attempted, but that one didn't sound musical to me. *Okay, let's look at some more bass riffs spotted In The Wild that use Passing Tones.*

The last note in each bar is syncopated, and there's an *elegant* chromatic run, from below:

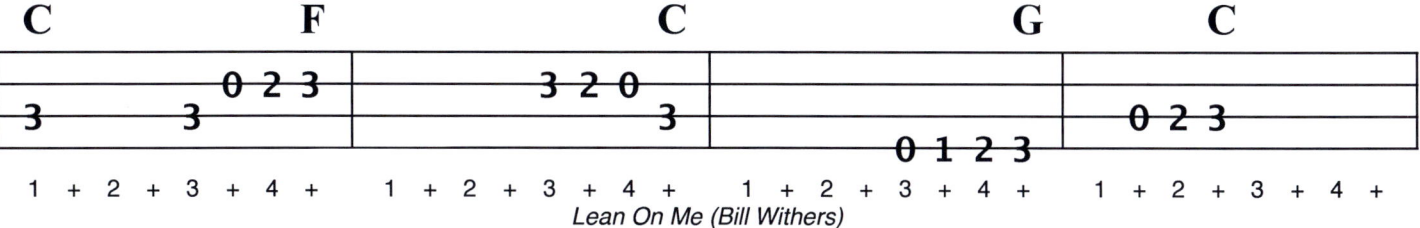
Lean On Me (Bill Withers)

Another little dip below the **Root**:

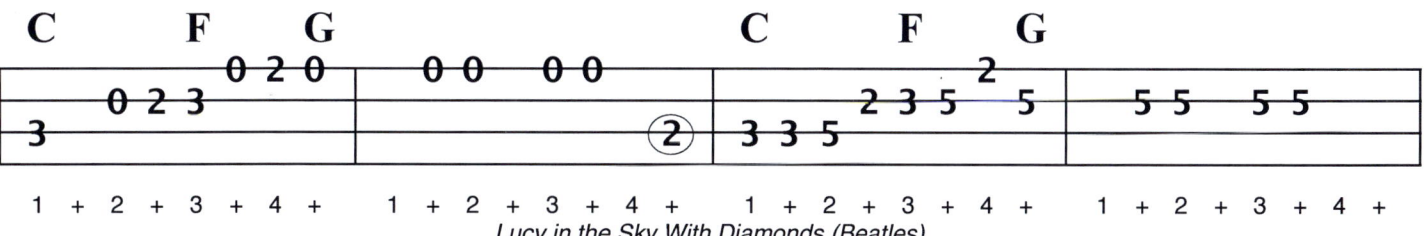
Lucy in the Sky With Diamonds (Beatles)

Of the next two, the first one has a syncopated note; otherwise, they're pretty similar:

La Bamba (Ritchie Valens)

Twist and Shout (Beatles)

Now in the **Key of G**, two riffs with the same notes but with such different feels:

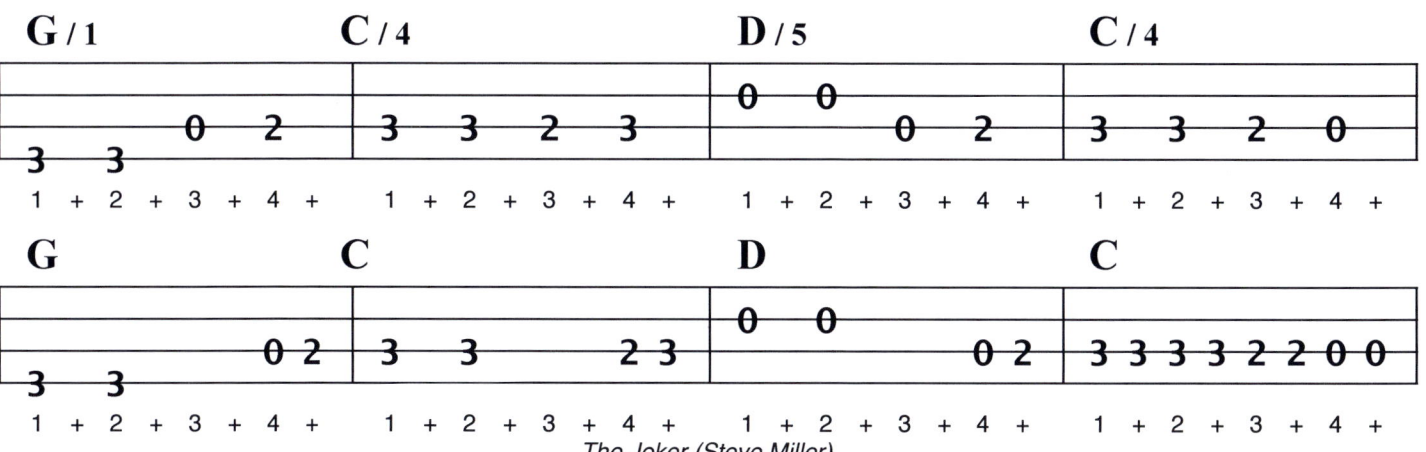
The Joker (Steve Miller)

I'm not big on playing mindless exercises, but this one in the **Key of A** might be good for memorizing the Ascending and Descending Universal Major Scale shape:

And this might be a fun application of that:

ABC (Jackson 5)

But after all that business, most of the time, you really only need to embellish lightly with the Major Scale. Here's another country progression, in the **Key of A**, that connects **Root Notes** a little more creatively than our first example, with **Hi** and **Lo 1 - 4 - 5**s and **Hi** and **Lo 5ths**:

Act Naturally (Beatles)

Minor Chords and the C Chord Family

As I mentioned earlier, we are obviously bouncing back and forth between
Note Issues (notes within scales & chords) and *Chord Issues* (chords within keys).
The Note Issues are brought to you by "**1 - 3 - 5**" and the *degrees* in the Major Scale.
The Chord Issues are brought to you by "**1 - 4 - 5**" and the *chords* in the Chord Family.
It's about time for us to pivot back to the Chord Family to take a look at the Big Picture.

We've actually come quite a distance without really needing to discuss the *Minor Triad*.
So many songs rely exclusively on Major chords, regardless of key or style of music.
But now it's time to see how the *Major Scale* gives rise to Minor Triads just as
readily as Major Triads. And it's **SO SIMPLE** to lay out the whole process.

Start, again, with our dependable old friend, the **C Major Scale**.
Now just do as I say, and nobody gets hurt.

Lay out about an octave *and a half* of the **C Major Scale**. *These are **notes**, not chords:*

C	D	E	F	G	A	B	C	D	E	F	G
1	2	3	4	5	6	7	8/1	2	3	4	5

The plan is to assemble these notes into *7 Triads*, each *Rooted* on a different degree.
From each **Triad Root Note**, we pick off the *1st, 3rd* and *5th* notes, leading to a **1 chord**,
a **2 chord**, a **3 chord** and so on. Starting with **C**, we spell out the **1 chord** in the **Key of C**:

1 chord: (C) D (E) F (G) A B C D E F = C - E - G

While we're at it, let's go ahead and do the same thing for the other 6 scale degrees.
Now, although the **D** note is the **2nd degree**, it's the *1st degree* of its own Triad. And so on:

2 chord: C (D) E (F) G (A) B C D E F = D - F - A

3 chord: C D (E) F (G) A (B) C D E F = E - G - B

4 chord: C D E (F) G (A) B (C) D E F = F - A - C

5 chord: C D E F (G) A (B) C (D) E F = G - B - D

6 chord: C D E F G (A) B (C) D (E) F = A - C - E

7 chord: C D E F G A (B) C (D) E (F) = B - D - F

Now you know why we extended the octave. Okay, I think all this is fascinating.....

The **1 chord** has a *Major Chord Quality*. Specifically, this means that the interval between *the 1st and 3rd degrees of the Triad is a **Major 3rd***, meaning that they are **4 Half-steps apart** (or 2 Whole-steps). For the **C** chord, the sequence of notes is **C - E - G**, and if you look at the Fretboard Diagram below, you can directly observe, on the **A/3rd** string, that 4-fret distance between the **C** note (3rd fret) and the **E** note (7th fret).

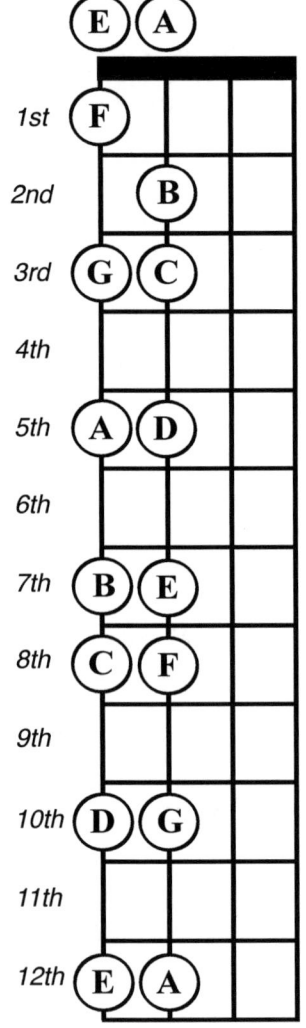

Well, this phenomenon is *also* true for the **4** and **5 chords**, **F** and **G**: All three chords have **4 Half-steps** from **Root** to **3rd**:

C	D	E		F	G	A		G	A	B
R	2nd	3rd		R	2nd	3rd		R	2nd	3rd
3	5	7		1	3	5		3	5	7

But this is definitely *not* what you see when you examine the **2, 3** and **6 chords**, the **D, E** and **A**:

D	E	F		E	F	G		A	B	C
R	2nd	3rd		R	2nd	3rd		R	2nd	3rd
5	7	8		7	8	10		5	7	8

For these Triads, the interval is **3 Half-steps** between **1st** and **3rd**. This is an interval of a **Minor 3rd**, and makes the whole Triad *Minor*.

*Point of Order: We'll refer to these as the **2m, 3m** and **6m chords**.*

That's about it. Now, there IS one more Triad in the Chord Family, the **7 chord**, that I have conveniently ignored. I knew you were going to ask about it. It's called a **Diminished Triad**, and it really won't be very useful to us, so I vote that we continue to ignore it.

If you're not sure how the Minor Chord Quality sounds, here are the patterns for our three Minor chords, **Dm, Em** and **Am**, in the **Key of C**. As expected, they all have the same shape:

E minor = E - G - B   A minor = A - C - E   D minor = D - F - A

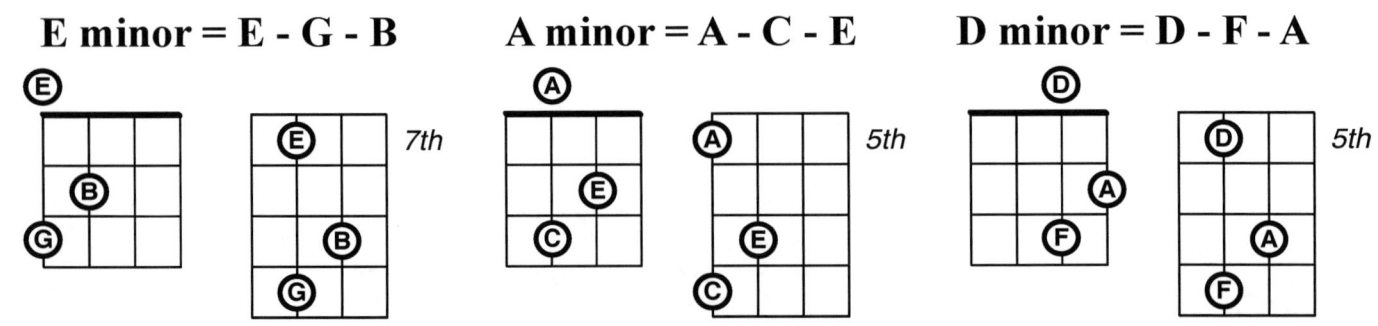

The G and D Chord Families

I want to run you through the same process for two more keys (seeing is believing). First up, the **Key of G**. Remember, **G** is a **Fifth** above **C** and it has *all the same notes except* for the F# instead of the F. All the other notes are natural notes for both keys:

G	A	B	C	D	E	F#	G	A	B	C	D
1	2	3	4	5	6	7	8/1	2	3	4	5

This time we lay out an octave and a half of the **G Major Scale** and count off the **1 - 3 - 5** Triads from each of *these* scale degrees, which have become **Triad Roots**:

1 chord: (G) A (B) C (D) E F# G A B C = G - B - D = **G**

2 chord: G (A) B (C) D (E) F# G A B C = A - C - E = **Am**

3 chord: G A (B) C (D) E (F#) G A B C = B - D - F# = **Bm**

4 chord: G A B (C) D (E) F# (G) A B C = C - E - G = **C**

5 chord: G A B C (D) E (F#) G (A) B C = D - F# - A = **D**

6 chord: G A B C D (E) F# (G) A (B) C = E - G - B = **Em**

This is where it gets a little messy, but it's far from impenetrable.....*But if this is NOT so interesting to you right now, you can come back later. Feel free to skip ahead a bit.*

Let's compare the chords from the two Chord Families that we've generated from the **C** and **G Major Scales**, which differ one from another by just 1 note out of 7:

I've circled the chords that these two keys have in common: **C, G, Am** and **Em** *(only four!)*. But the **Key of C** *alone* has the **F** and **Dm** chords and the **Key of G** *alone* has the **Bm** and **D**.

This is all due to a difference of *just one note*, **F** in the **Key of C** versus **F#** note in the **Key of G**. Now consider the **D** Triads:

In the **Key of C**, it's 3 Half-steps from **D** to **F**. It's a **Minor 3rd**.
In the **Key of G**, it's 4 Half-steps from **D** to **F#**. It's a **Major 3rd**.

So applying this process to the **D** note in each key generates a **Minor Triad** in the **Key of C** and a **Major Triad** in the **Key of G**.

Chord	Key	Key
1	(C)	(G)
2	Dm	(Am)
3	(Em)	Bm
4	F	(C)
5	(G)	D
6	(Am)	(Em)

Just one more of these exercises, this time for the **Key of D**. Remember, **D** is a **Fifth** above **G** and it has *one more sharp, the C#, added to the F# we found in the Key of G*:

D	E	(F#)	G	A	B	(C#)	D	E	(F#)	G	A
1	2	3	4	5	6	7	8/1	2	3	4	5

1 chord: (D) E (F#) G (A) B C# D E F# G = D - F# - A = **D**

2 chord: D (E) F# (G) A (B) C# D E F# G = E - G - B = **Em**

3 chord: D E (F#) G (A) B (C#) D E F# G = F# - A - C# = **F#m**

4 chord: D E F# (G) A (B) C# (D) E F# G = G - B - D = **G**

5 chord: D E F# G (A) B (C#) D (E) F# G = A - C# - E = **A**

6 chord: D E F# G A (B) C# (D) E (F#) G = B - D - F# = **Bm**

Now let's compare the members of the **C**, **G** and **D** Chord Families:

Sorry, you can't turn back now! Look, I put squares around the four chords that the **Keys of G** and **D** share, which happen to be **G**, **D**, **Em** and **Bm**. Fine.

But here's the fascinating bit: Look at the **G** column. *There are only 2 chords that have both a circle and a square around them: the G and the Em chords.*

Chord	Key	Key	Key
1	(C)	[G]	D
2	Dm	(Am)	[Em]
3	(Em)	[Bm]	F#m
4	F	(C)	[G]
5	(G)	[D]	A
6	(Am)	[(Em)]	Bm

*So those are the only chords that the **Keys of C** and **D** share.* These keys are *two Fifths* away from each other, so they are farther apart *musically* than either is from the **Key of G**.

The Keys of C and D differ by only 2 sharps, **F#** and **C#**, but that's enough to ensure that they have *only 2 chords in common*. Here's a nifty analogy: YOU are the **Key of G**. You have cousins (the **Key of C**) on your paternal side as well as cousins (the **Key of D**) on your maternal side who may not even know about each other, but you are related to both sets of cousins to the same degree. Well, it's not a perfect analogy, but you get the picture.

(If you go up a **Fifth** from **D**, you find **A**, and if you compare the **Keys of C** and **A**, they differ by a measly 3 sharps and yet have NO CHORDS in common.)

What this is all leading up to is......I forget, why did I go through all that? Oh yeah.

This is the Big Picture of Music. There are 12 keys, one for each note in the Chromatic Scale. We extract the Major Scale from the Chromatic scale by "2 Wholes and a Half, 3 Wholes and a Half," and then use the 7 Major Scale degrees to generate the Major and Minor chords that form the basis for all the music in Western Civilization. And keys that are closer in their number of accidentals share more chords.

Were I to push you through the Chord Family Shuffle for the **Keys of A** and **E**, you'd find that we would add the **G#** note and the **C#m** chord to the **Key of A** and the **D#** note and **G#m** chord to the **Key of E**. I needn't rub your nose in it, eh?

For the **C-A-G-E-D keys**, *THIS* is all you need to know (I flipped the axes on the chart):

Remember, I left out the chord that forms at the **7th** degree, called the **Half-diminished**.

Chord / Key	1	2m	3m	4	5	6m
C	**C**	**Dm**	**Em**	**F**	**G**	**Am**
G	**G**	**Am**	**Bm**	**C**	**D**	**Em**
D	**D**	**Em**	**F#m**	**G**	**A**	**Bm**
A	**A**	**Bm**	**C#m**	**D**	**E**	**F#m**
E	**E**	**F#m**	**G#m**	**A**	**B**	**C#m**

One very practical lesson that you can glean from the above chart is that you can't simply "count letters" when you're looking for Minor chords. For example, if you're in the **Key of D** and you need the **3 chord**, you can't just count **1 - 2 - 3**, oh, that's **D - E - F**. No, that's only a **Minor 3rd**, and you need to go up one more fret to **F#**. And the **6 chord** in the **Key of E** is **C#m**, not **Cm**.

Just as Uhura, Sulu and Chekov have different functions on the *Enterprise* bridge, so do the three Minor chords in the Chord Family. *The most important of the three is the **6m**, so important that it has a special designation, the **Relative Minor**.*

You know, the Minor chords don't show up nearly as often as the Major chords, but when one does, there's at least a 50% chance that it'll be the Relative Minor. One of the more common chord progressions is: **1 - 6m - 4 - 5**, and that'll be the first one we will run through the **C-A-G-E-D** Chord Families.

The next most important Minor chord is the **2m**, especially in its role in one type of chord progression called the **Rhythm Changes** (after the song "I Got Rhythm"), which is: **1 - 6m - 2m - 5** (not too different from the **1 - 6m - 4 - 5** above) and in another one called the **Jazz Turnaround**, simply: **2m - 5 - 1**. You'll see.

The **3m**? Sort of the black sheep of the Chord Family, although the Beatles loved it.

Let's get in some practice playing the **1 - 6m - 4 - 5**. Since we're adding a new Chord Quality, let's start off simply with the **Triad Root Note** locations.

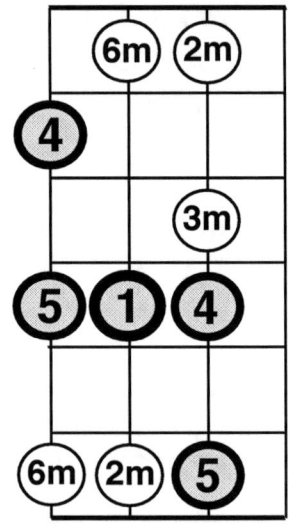

The diagram to the *left* should look familiar. There's the skeleton of the **1 - 4 - 5 Root Notes** that we saw before, which has (1) the **Key Root** on the *A/3rd string* and (2) both the Lower and the Upper **Roots** for the **4** and **5** chords.

All we've done is to add the nearby **Roots** for the **2m**, **3m** and **6m chords**.

Similarly, to the *right* you see the situation for the **Key Root** located on the *E/4th string*, with only Upper **Roots** for the **4** and **5 chords**.

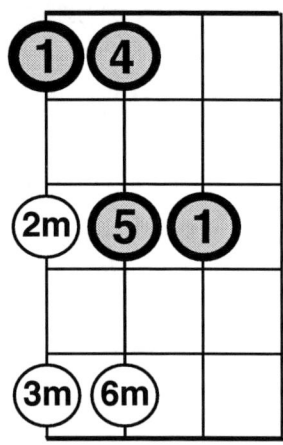

The **Key of D** can serve as an example for all the keys with their **Roots** on the **A/3rd** string (**C, D, E, F, G** and accidentals). The **6m chord** in the **Key of D** is **Bm**, and we'll look at two positions for that **B** note: *3rd string/2nd fret* and *4th string/7th fret*. Here's a CRG:

```
 D / 1       Bm / 6m      G / 4     A / 5        D          Bm          G           A
|                       |                      |                       |
| 5      5 2  2         |                      | 5         5           |
|                       |  3    3 5   5        |              7    7   | 3     3 5    5
|                       |                      |                       |
  1 + 2 + 3 + 4 +        1 + 2 + 3 + 4 +        1 + 2 + 3 + 4 +         1 + 2 + 3 + 4 +
```

In the first case, you can play the whole thing in 2nd Position: 4th finger on the **D Root**, 1st finger on the **B**, etc. In the second case, you might as well start off with the 1st finger in 5th Position, then shift down to **G** in 3rd Position.

The **Key of A** can serve as an example for all the keys with their **Roots** on the **E/4th** string (**G, A, B, C, D** and accidentals). (The 2nd one starts at the Octave and goes down for the **6m**.)

```
 A / 1       F#m / 6m     D / 4     E / 5        A          F#m         D           E
|                       |                      |  7        7 4   4     |
|         4     4       |                      |     9         9       |            
|   9        9          |  5    5 7   7        |                       | 5     5 7    7
| 5       5             |                      |                       |
  1 + 2 + 3 + 4 +        1 + 2 + 3 + 4 +        1 + 2 + 3 + 4 +         1 + 2 + 3 + 4 +
```

This is where I'm supposed to tell you, "Be creative!" and you should be, if you feel like it. Look what I found, just cruising around the neck with these **Triad Root** patterns in mind:

```
|                       |                      |                       | 7     7 9    9
|                       |                      |  7       7 4   4      |
|                       |  5    5 7   7        |                       |
| 5       5 2  2        |                      |                       |
  1 + 2 + 3 + 4 +        1 + 2 + 3 + 4 +        1 + 2 + 3 + 4 +         1 + 2 + 3 + 4 +
```

Here's a sampling of some songs that contain a **1 - 6m - 4 - 5** chord progression:

*Blue Moon   Unchained Melody   I Will Always Love You   Stand By Me
Where Have All The Flowers Gone   All I Have To Do Is Dream   YMCA
Stay (Just a Little Bit Longer)   Crocodile Rock   Every Breath You Take*

Before we go any farther, let's expand that **6m Root Note** into a whole Triad.

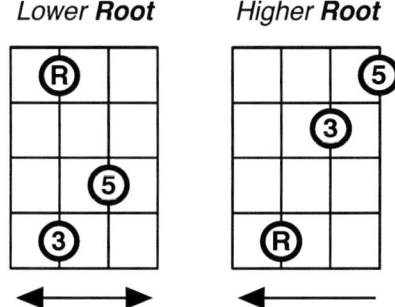

You will generally see two different shapes for Minor Triads. The first shape to the right is to be used when the **Triad Root** is *lower on the neck* than the **3rd** and **5th**, so the 1st finger gets it.

The second shape works when the **Triad Root** is *higher on the neck* than the **3rd** and **5th**, so the 4th finger gets it. And both shapes can be shifted to higher or lower sets of strings.

We'll expand all the **Roots** for the **1 - 6m - 4 - 5**s above into **3rds**, **5ths** and **8ths**, Clave-style. The first one (**Key of D**) has all Triads, and we use the Minor chord shape with the Lower **Root**:

D / 1   **Bm / 2m**   **G / 4**   **A / 5**

```
---4---7----------|----------4-------|------------------|------------------
-5----------------|--2---5-----------|--2---5-----------|--4---7-----------
------------------|------------------|-3----------------|-5----------------
```
1 + 2 + 3 + 4 +   1 + 2 + 3 + 4 +   1 + 2 + 3 + 4 +   1 + 2 + 3 + 4 +

Here the **D** and **A** chords both go **Root - 5th**, plus the Minor shape with the Higher **Root**:

D   **Bm**   **G**   **A**

```
------------------|----------4-------|------------------|------------------
-5------5---------|-5----------------|------2---5-------|--7-------5-------
----5-------------|----7-------------|-3----------------|------5-----------
```
1 + 2 + 3 + 4 +   1 + 2 + 3 + 4 +   1 + 2 + 3 + 4 +   1 + 2 + 3 + 4 +

Now in the **Key of A**, it's all Triads, and the Minor shape with the Higher **Root**:

A / 1   **F#m / 6m**   **D / 4**   **E / 5**

```
------------------|--------6---------|------------------|----------6---9---
----4---7---------|------7-----------|------4---7-------|--7---------------
-5----------------|--9---------------|-5----------------|------------------
```
1 + 2 + 3 + 4 +   1 + 2 + 3 + 4 +   1 + 2 + 3 + 4 +   1 + 2 + 3 + 4 +

Here the **A** chord goes **Root - 5th**, the **F#m** has the Higher Root, and **D** and **E** go **Root - 3rd**:

A   **F#m**   **D**   **E**

```
------------------|--------6---------|------------------|----------6-------
-7------7---------|--7---7-----------|------4-----------|--7---------7-----
----7-------------|------9-----------|-5--------5-------|------7-----------
```
1 + 2 + 3 + 4 +   1 + 2 + 3 + 4 +   1 + 2 + 3 + 4 +   1 + 2 + 3 + 4 +

Let's take the **6m** down to Open Position in the **Key of C**. The first two bars use the open **A** note, and the repeat uses both the **A** and **G**. This is all Triads.

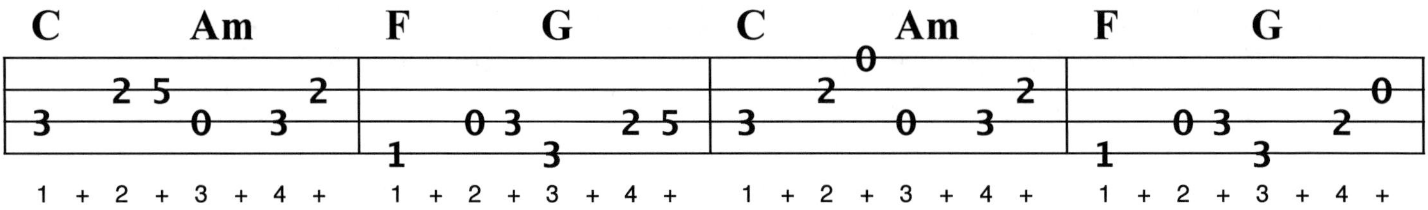

D'yer Mak'er (Led Zeppelin)

Many of the **1 - 6m - 4 - 5** examples In The Wild use passing tones to connect the **Roots**. This one is in the **Key of A**, and makes repeated use of the **7th** degree of the scale, the **G#** note:

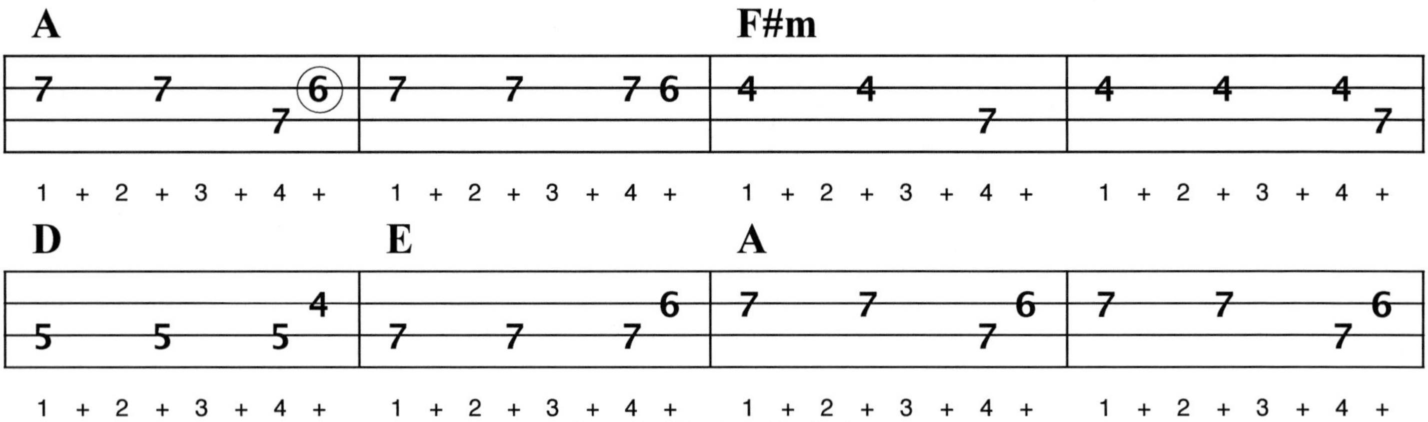

Stand By Me (Ben E. King)

This next riff, also in the **Key of A**, runs through the same changes double-time, and in the repeat, it substitutes a **Bm** where the **D** should be. More on that shortly.

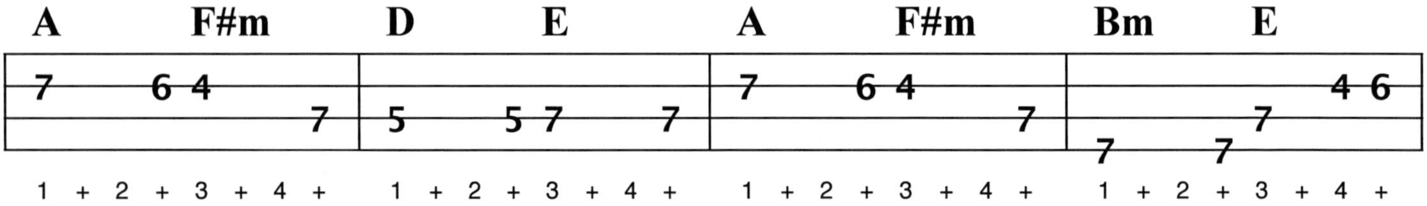

I Will Always Love You (Whitney Houston)

In the two examples above, we used just the **Root** of the **6m**, but in the next one (**Key of E**), we use the Triad. Liberties are taken in the repeat. *Try it in 4th Position (start with 4th finger):*

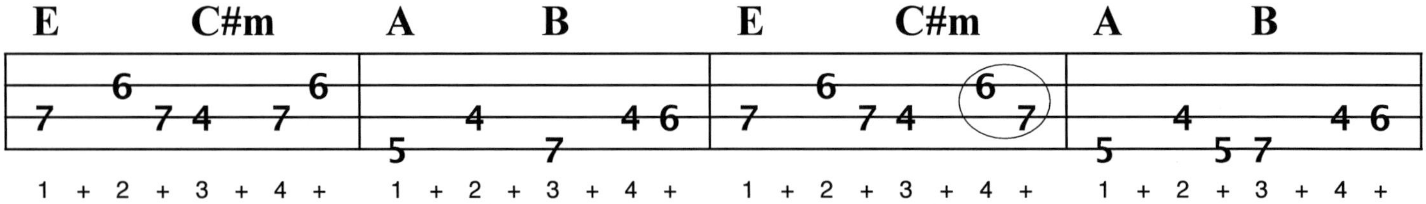

All I Have To Do Is Dream (Everly Brothers)

Here are two more takes on it. The first one goes high and the second one goes high, then low.

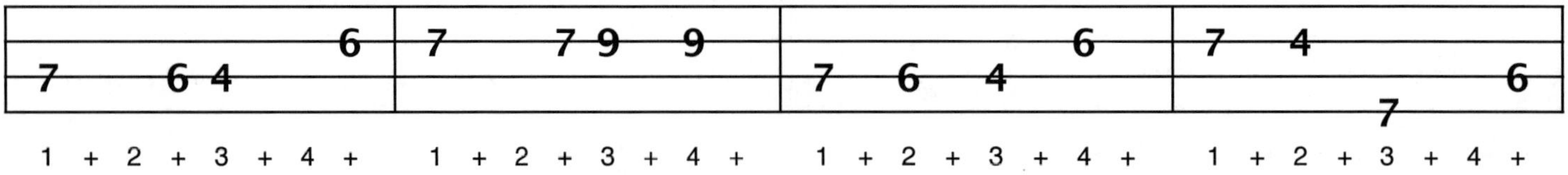

While the **1 - 6m - 4 - 5** progression is popular and powerful, it's by no means the only way to introduce the **6m** to the **1 - 4 - 5**. Here are some other ways, in **D**:

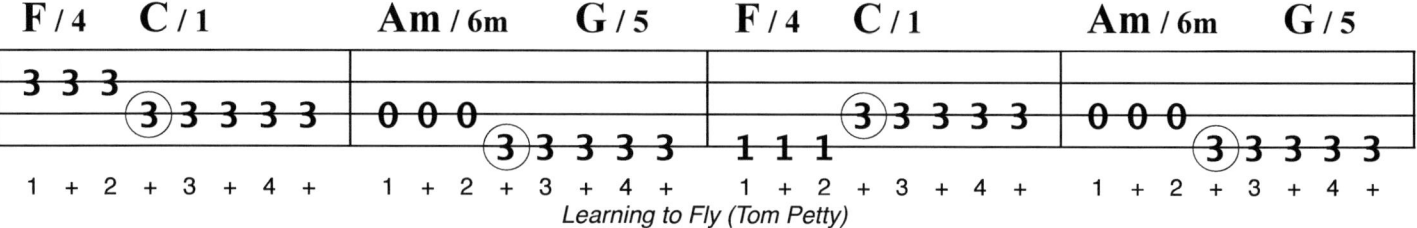

With or Without You (U2)

Baby, It's You (Beatles)

This one starts on the **4 chord (Key of C)** and some of the chord changes are syncopated:

Learning to Fly (Tom Petty)

And this one starts on the **6m chord**, dwells on the **4 chord** for a bit and finally gets around to the **1 chord** by the 4th measure. All that, and more, in the **Key of D**:

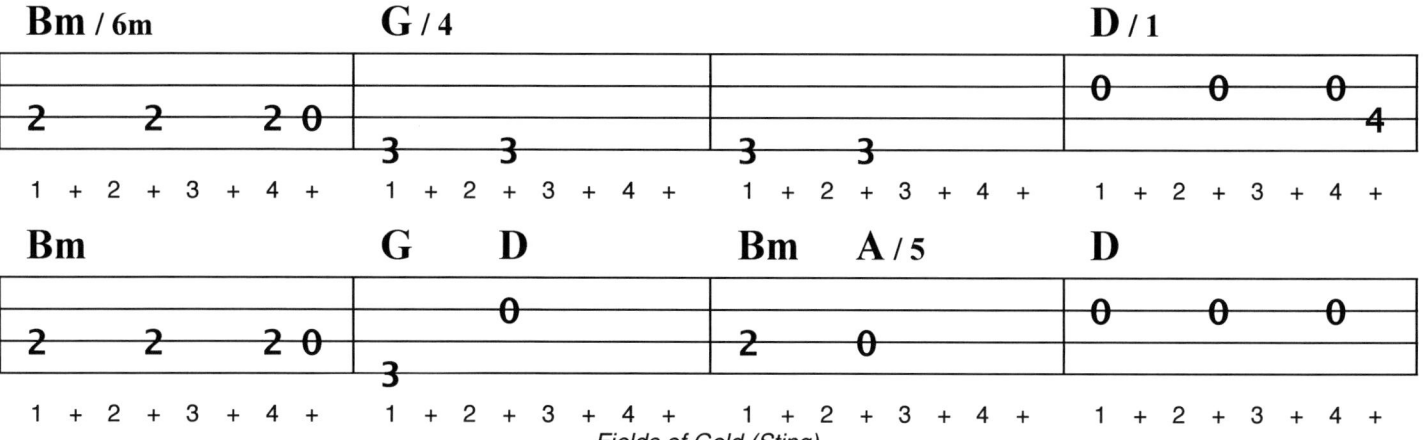

Fields of Gold (Sting)

55

The 2m Chord and the Rhythm Changes
(1 - 6m - 2m - 5)

This is one of the most confusing terms in music that you'll EVER hear. The term "The Rhythm Changes" refers to a chord progression that starts off the Gershwin song, "I Got Rhythm." There's no direct connection between this term and the rhythmic beat inherent in music. It might have been called "The Banana Changes" had the song, "Yes, We Have No Bananas" begun with this chord progression. Sheesh.

Obviously, the only difference between this and the **1 - 6m - 4 - 5** changes is that the **2m chord** in the Chord Family takes the place of the **4 chord**. Don't worry, it's okay and it makes perfect sense (to me) because if you take the **4 chord** and make it the **1 chord** in its own key, then the **2m chord** becomes the **6m chord** in the new key, which is (ta-da) the Relative Minor!

Don't worry. Just know that the **4** and **2m chords** substitute for each other nicely. The **4 chord** is favored more by the Rockers and the **2m chord** more by the Jazzers.

Trade the **2m (Em)** for the **4 chord** in the **Key of D**, using the **Key Root** on the **A/3rd** string:

```
  D / 1         Bm / 6m       Em / 2m      A / 5        D             Bm            Em            A
|                           |   2     2               |                           |                          |
|                           |                         |                           |   7     7                |
|  5      5  2    2         |               5    5    |  5     5                  |               5    5    |
|                           |         5  5            |          7     7          |   7     7                |
  1 + 2 + 3 + 4 +    1 + 2 + 3 + 4 +    1 + 2 + 3 + 4 +    1 + 2 + 3 + 4 +
```

Do the same thing in the **Key of A (Bm is the 2m)**, using the **Key Root** on the **E/4th** string:

```
  A / 1        F#m / 6m      Bm / 2m       E / 5        A            F#m           Bm            E
|                           |                         |   7     7                 |   9     9                |
|           4     4         |                         |           9     9         |                          |
|                           |           7     7       |                           |               7    7    |
|  5     5                  |  7    7                 |                           |                          |
  1 + 2 + 3 + 4 +    1 + 2 + 3 + 4 +    1 + 2 + 3 + 4 +    1 + 2 + 3 + 4 +
```

Might as well get the Triads out of the way as well. Here they are in the **Key of D**:

```
  D / 1                     Bm / 2m                   Em / 2m                                A / 5
|                           |                         |                     4                |
|          4     7          |             4           |   2    5                              |             4     7
|  5                        |   2    5                |                                       |                         
|                           |                         |                                       |  5                      
  1 + 2 + 3 + 4 +    1 + 2 + 3 + 4 +    1 + 2 + 3 + 4 +    1 + 2 + 3 + 4 +
```

```
|                           |                         |                4                    |
|                           |             4           |   5                                 |
|                           |                         |        7                             |           7
|  5         5              |   5                     |                                     |                     
|       5                   |        7                |                                     |  5            5     
  1 + 2 + 3 + 4 +    1 + 2 + 3 + 4 +    1 + 2 + 3 + 4 +    1 + 2 + 3 + 4 +
```

Now the Rhythm Changes in the **Key of A**:

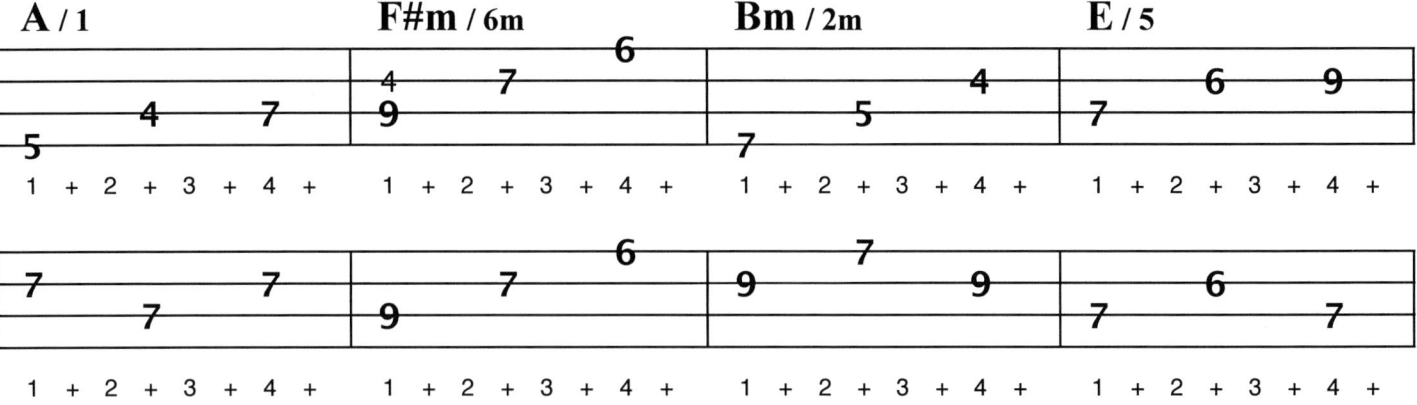

Let's look at some examples. Unless I tell you otherwise, the first chord in any of these progressions is the **1 chord**, the Key Chord.

The first line needs too much muting; ah, but the second one sends me:

You Send Me (Sam Cooke)

This one has a chromatic "approach" note that comes from outside the key: the **4**, a C#.

Sherry (Four Seasons)

Talk about approach notes! Here's one for every chord change, with 2 chromatic Passing Tones starting on **Count 4**. From **C** to **Am**, they come from below, and for the next two changes, to **Dm** then G, they come from above. Sounds suspiciously *jazzy*.

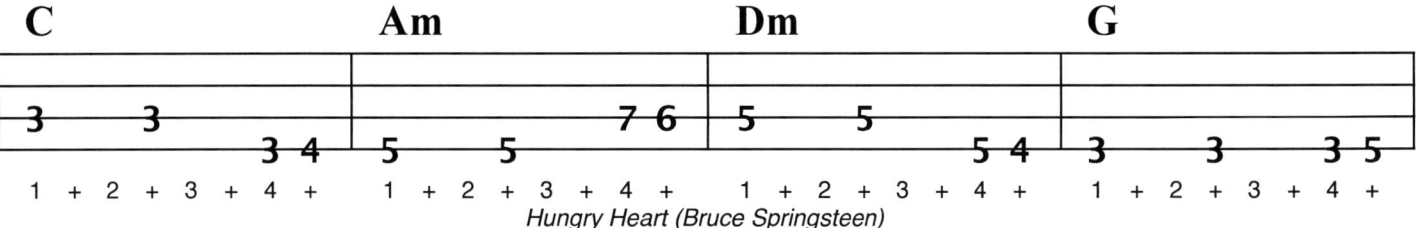

Hungry Heart (Bruce Springsteen)

Another example of the Rhythm Changes with Passing Tones in the **Key of E**:

```
E / 1      C#m / 6m   F#m / 2m   B / 5       E          C#m        F#m        B
                                                                              4  6  4
 2 2                                          2 2                             
        3 4 4                    4 2 2 4 2          3 4 4                 4 2
                          4    2 2                                4     2 2
 1 + 2 + 3 + 4 +   1 + 2 + 3 + 4 +    1 + 2 + 3 + 4 +    1 + 2 + 3 + 4 +
                   You Make Me Feel Like Dancing (Leo Sayer)
```

I mentioned the **Jazz Turnaround** back along; seems pretty innocuous, this **2m - 5 - 1**. But jazz composers make great use of this little progression to establish a key feeling or to confirm a key change. Although such issues are beyond the scope of this book, you at least have some experience with this small-but-large piece of jazz theory.

The 3m Chord

I called the **3m** chord the black sheep of the Chord Family because it just doesn't seem to have a distinct voice. But it has a significant role in one progression: the **1 - 2m - 3m - 4** (and sometimes **5**). It amounts to walking up the Major Scale and catching a chord for each scale degree. It's not commonly played, but it's nice, something like this:

```
C / 1      Dm / 2m    Em / 3m   F / 4        G / 5
               0         0    2     2 3    3     5     5 5     5     5     5 5     5
 3       3
 1 + 2 + 3 + 4 +   1 + 2 + 3 + 4 +    1 + 2 + 3 + 4 +    1 + 2 + 3 + 4 +
                   Like a Rolling Stone (Bob Dylan)
```

Or in reverse, starting on the **4 chord**:

```
F          Em         Dm        C           F          Em         Dm         C
 3       3 2      2    0       0   0 2       3       3 2      2    0 2 3    0 2
                               3                                       3
 1 + 2 + 3 + 4 +   1 + 2 + 3 + 4 +    1 + 2 + 3 + 4 +    1 + 2 + 3 + 4 +
                   Best of My Love (The Emotions)
```

As I say, the Beatles liked the **3m chord** and used it extensively, and it certainly has an unexpected sound, a sort of bittersweet version of the **1 chord**, and I do believe that John and Paul managed to find some interesting places to insert it. Such as:

```
G / 1                 D / 5              Em / 6m             Bm / 3m        D
 5    5    5
         5            5    5 5 4 5 6    7    7 7    7                        5
                                                              7    7 7
 1 + 2 + 3 + 4 +   1 + 2 + 3 + 4 +    1 + 2 + 3 + 4 +    1 + 2 + 3 + 4 +
                   I Want To Hold Your Hand (Beatles)
```

The Circle of Fifths

For many people who have dabbled in music, the expression **"The Circle of Fifths"** inspires abject fear and loathing, and encourages a hasty and disorderly retreat into other walks of life. I think it's been used as a scare tactic, or at least as an instrument of exclusion, an artificial raising of the bar to restrict membership. Really, once you get it, you wonder, "Is that all there is to it?" Maybe that's why musicians protect it so. That being said, this stuff takes a bit of penetration, so feel free to skip ahead to the playing.

If you have no fear of a thorough yet easy-to-read explanation of the Circle, I'll remind you of my **Music Principles for the Skeptical Guitarist, Volume One**. Here, I just want to feed you the tasty results without boring you with the recipe.

I love it when some music method book plasters a picture of the Circle of Fifths right on the first page, as if to say, "Get back, honky cat, music is so very harrrd!!" True, Music is not a dawdle. But as I've said before, if I can get it, *you* can get it. Anyway, I'm holding back on showing you the actual Circle until we can talk.....

Here's the long / short of it. Remember that chart from 8 pages ago? I've added *two more keys*, and here's the result:

To review: You start with the **Key of C**, with no accidentals, and you start going through the Musical Alphabet by **Fifths**. Each new key contains (1) the sharps from the last key and (2) a new one. Here's the executive version of it:

Chord	1	2m	3m	4	5	6m
C	C	Dm	Em	F	G	Am
G	G	Am	Bm	C	D	Em
D	D	Em	F#m	G	A	Bm
A	A	Bm	C#m	D	E	F#m
E	E	F#m	G#m	A	B	C#m
B	B	C#m	D#m	E	F#	G#m
F#	F#	G#m	A#m	B	C#	D#m

C D E F **G** A B C **D** E F#G **A** B C#D **E** F#G#A **B** C#D#E **F#** etc.

Before, we stopped at the **Key of E**, which has 4 sharps. Well, now we go up a **5th**, and the **Key of B** has 5 sharps, and up another **5th**, and the **Key of F#** has 6 sharps.

What does this all mean? *As you proceed by **5ths** away from C, each new key has fewer and fewer notes in common with C, and is therefore **less related** to the **Key of C**.* In fact, the key that is next up from **F#** is the **Key of C#**---it's *all sharp* notes, whereas the **Key of C** is *all natural* notes---these two keys have NOTHING in common. It's all about *cousins of cousins of cousins*. The closer two keys are by **5ths**, the more closely related and the more friendly they are with each other.

Okay, we're only interested in the Big Letters now, not how they were generated. And these letters pose the Eternal Question:

Can't **G**irls **D**o **A**nything **E**lse **B**ut **F**lirt?

It also works this way, Ladies:

Can't **G**uys **D**o **A**nything **E**lse **B**ut **F**lirt?

So this is the sequence of all the sharp keys as you move *Upward by Fifths*.

But guess what: *Music wants to travel* **Downward** *by Fifths. Doh!*

It doesn't matter why; it wants what it wants.
It has to do with, like, you know, physics and stuff.
I mean, why do you want what *you* want, man?

Anyway, it turns out that the *reverse* of the **CGDAEBF#** is going to be more useful to us:

Fling Bruce Emery's Amplifier Down the Grand Canyon

(Some have suggested flinging something else of mine down there. How indelicate!)

You're going to love how all this mess comes back around and kisses you on the cheek.

Remember all those examples of the Rhythm Changes in different keys?
Take a look at the sequences of the chords.......if you dare......:

Key of C: "Sherry"	(C) **Am Dm G C**	*Amp Down the Grand Canyon*
Key of G: "You Send Me"	(G) **Em Am D G**	*Emery's Amp Down the Grand*
Key of D: 3rd-string Examples	(D) **Bm Em A D**	*Bruce Emery's Amp Down*
Key of A: 4th-string Examples	(A) **F#m Bm E A**	*Fling Bruce Emery's Amp*
Key of E: "You Make Me..."	(E) **C#m F#m B E**	*C'mon, Fling Bruce Emery!*

If this doesn't thrill you, you might possibly have a heart of stone.
This is the best reality show *EVER*. Whew, I'm exhausted! In a good way.

(As for the "C'mon", I did mention that the **Key of C#** is the next line after **F#**.....)

So this sequence of keys & chords cuts across the boundaries of the provincial,
narrow-minded Chord Family and ties together the entire Musical Galaxy.

And it's called a *Circle* of **Fifths** because, if you travel *down* a **Fifth** from the **Key of C** (because frequencies go down as well as up, forever), you run smack into the *Key of F*, *which has 1 flat*. Aha! So that's why we bother keeping those old flat notes around!
Then you keep going down by **Fifths** and keep adding flats. Then the sharp and
flat keys meet up straight across the circle from the **Key of C**. Behold:

What it all boils down to is this: Regardless of what *key* you are playing in, and regardless of what *chord* within that key you are playing *on*, you will feel a (resistable) tug to travel to the chord that is Downward by a Fifth.

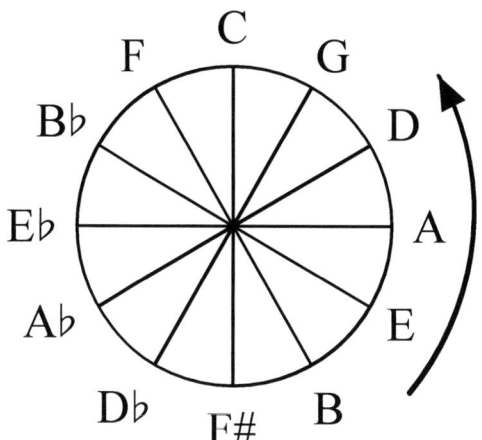

This process is called **backcycling** (people also say "Cycle of Fifths"), and it doesn't matter whether the chord is Major, Minor, 7th, 13th, whatever. Just follow the arrow back down through the keys (counter-clockwise).

Clearly, you don't *need* to respond to this pull, because usually we do not. But if we do, emotionally, it will seem like the right thing to have done.

I'm going on and on about this because, the more complexity in music you are exposed to, the more backcycling you're going to notice. This will hold truer for older music. So many of the old jazz standards are constructed from little bits of the Circle (such as the **2m - 5 - 1** Jazz Turnaround), that are used for moving from key to key with both interest and ease.

So we were talking about the Rhythm Changes. Say the **Key** is **C**. To play the **Am** chord is to reach up in the Circle and grab the **A** note, also known as the **5th** of the **5th** of the **5th** (since **G** is the **5th** of **C**, so **D** is the **5th** of the **5th** of **C**, so **A** is another **5th** away from **C**), and you just ride it down from **Am** to **Dm** to **G** to **C**. And the bassist plays the **Roots**.

There's just one complicating issue: Chord Quality. The **C** chord will be Major. The **G** chord can be either a Major or a **Seventh** chord. We haven't talked about those yet, and technically they're "flatted" Seventh chords (**b7th**), though we can just say "Seventh." But Seventh chords are based on a Major Triad, so we can deal with them as we would a Major Triad.

Ah, but both the **2** and the **6 chord** can appear in a song as *any* of the three chord types we've mentioned, Major, Minor or Seventh. Now, if the bassist wants to accompany these chords with just the **Root**, or the **Root** and the **5th**, then there's no problem. *But if you want to work in the 3rd, you need to know whether the chord is a happy Major or a sad Minor chord so you can choose the appropriate 3rd.* Just be aware.

How about the *5th* of the **5th** of the **5th** of the **5th**? That's four **5ths** away from the **Root**! Is that legit? Well, you'll never guess in a hundred years---that's that weird **3m chord**! And yes, it can work in backcycling, as either a Minor, Major or Seventh chord.

There is even a song that goes to (deep breath)
the 5th of the 5th of the 5th of the 5th of the 5th.
"Mister Sandman."

"Mister Sandman" is all Seventh chords, but all the bassist needs are the **Root Notes**. *Notice the characteristic zigzag pattern from* ***Triad Root*** *to* ***Root***. (And the word **BEAD**.)

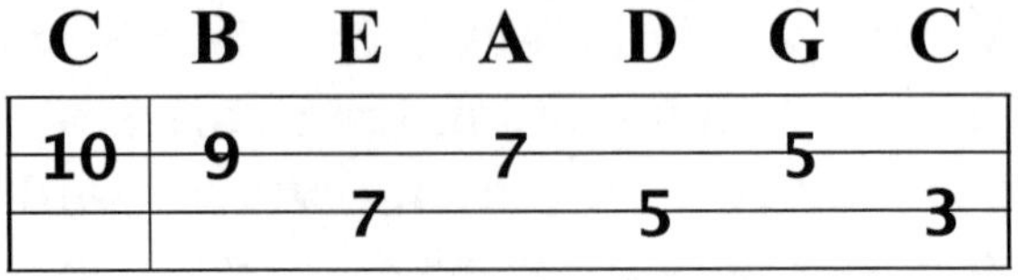

Try "Mister Sandman" with a **Root - 5th** bassline. Higher **5ths** alternate with lower **5ths**:

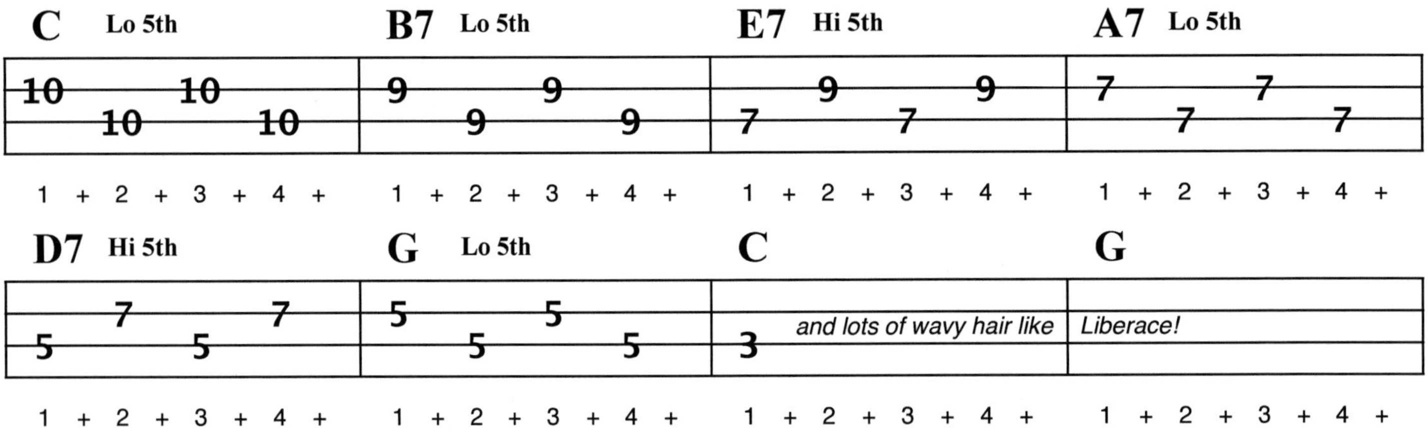

You will rarely travel through all these **5ths** in a row like this, but you'll see snippets. The trick is to know when you have found yourself inside one of these "wormholes," then once you know it, you can follow the zigzag pathway back out the other end.

Try two more with Seventh chords in two different keys (the second one has Triads):

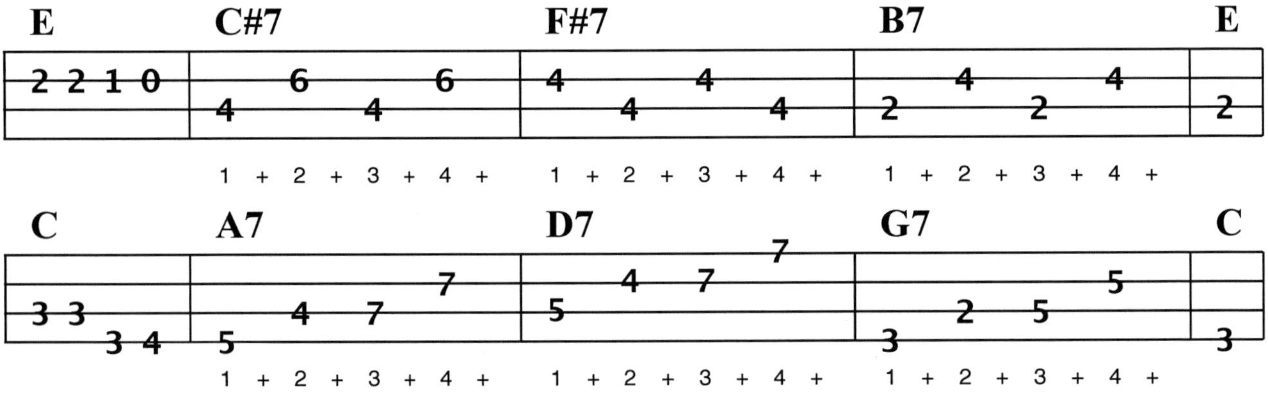

Here's a progression in the **Key of G** that jumps up to the 4th level of **5ths** and includes *all 6 chords in the* ***C Chord Family****:* ***1 - 2m - 3m - 4 - 5 - 6m*** (of course, not in that order). To do this, I had to cheat a little and step out of the Circle near the end to get the **4 chord** in:

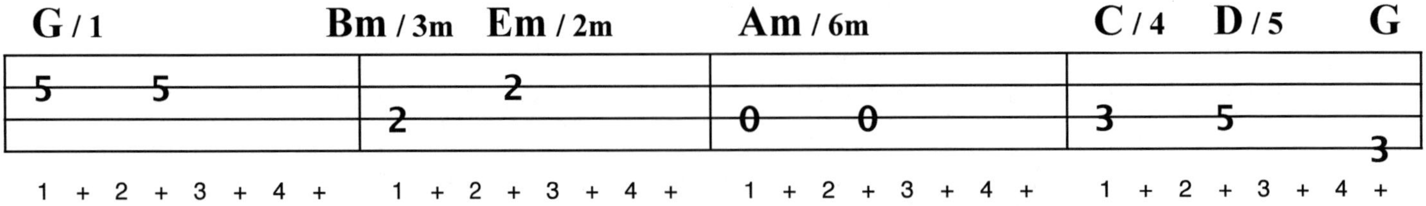

It's not *really* cheating; in the **Key of C**, the **C** and **Am** chords are Relative Major and Minor to each other, so they can substitute for each other anywhere else as well.

This one, in the **Key of C**, has one Minor chord mixed in with a number of Sevenths:

```
  C                  F     E7        Am       D7       G7       C
|-----------------|-----------------|------7-------|------5----------|
|-----------------|------8-----7----|-----------5--|-----------3-----|
|--8-----8-----8--|-----------------|--------------|-----------------|
  1 + 2 + 3 + 4 +   1 + 2 + 3 + 4 +  1 + 2 + 3 + 4 + 1 + 2 + 3 + 4 +
                     Don't Know Why (Norah Jones)
```

Let's finish up the Circle of Fifths with some Christmas cheer. The first two carols jump only to the Second Notch, **E7**, the **5th of the 5th**. (Just going to the **5 chord** is the First Notch.)

```
  D                    A     D              E7           A7
|-5----5-5---5----|----------5----5--|--5-------7--7---|-----------------|
|-----------------|-----5---5-5------|--------------5--|--5-----5-5---5--|
  1 + 2 + 3 + 4 +   1 + 2 + 3 + 4 +    1 + 2 + 3 + 4 +   1 + 2 + 3 + 4 +
  On the 5th day of Christmas my   true love gave to me   Five    golden     rings

  D                  A7    D            G       D         E7          A7
|-5-5-5---5-5-5---|--5--------5----5-|----------5---5-5-|--7----7--7------|
|-----------------|--------5--5------|--3----3--3-------|-----------5---5-|
  1 + 2 + 3 + 4 +   1 + 2 + 3 + 4 +    1 + 2 + 3 + 4 +   1 + 2 + 3 + 4 +
  Jingle bells,  Jingle Bells   Jingle   all the way   Oh, what fun it is to ride in a   one horse open sleigh
```

This next one flies right to the Third notch, **B7**, the **5th of the 5th of the 5th**, settles down a **5th** to **Em**, but then does *not* proceed to **A7** as expected. Life is full of disappointment.

```
  D         B7       Em        G        D         A7       D
|-5---------------|-----7-----------|--5--------------|--5--------------|
|-------7---------|----------3------|-----------5-----|-----------------|
  1 + 2 + 3 + 4 +   1 + 2 + 3 + 4 +   1 + 2 + 3 + 4 +   1 + 2 + 3 + 4 +
  Oh, little town of   Bethlehem       how    Still  we   see   thee    lie
```

This last one is an entire Associate Degree in Backcycling. You start, harmlessly enough, with the **1 chord**, **D**, and mosey over to visit the **4 chord**, **G**, no biggie. Then you leap up a couple Notches to **E7**, and settle down a **5th** to **A7**; interesting enough. Then, without *any* warning, you shoot up another *4 Notches*, grab the 5th of the blah blah blah, **F#7**, and ride it all the way home, **BEAD**. That's like a double axel into a triple lutz!

```
  D      G          E7     A7        F#7      Bm         Em    A7   D
|-5---------------|-----7-----------|--9--------------|------7----5-----|
|-------3---------|-----------5-----|----------7------|--------------5--|
  We wish you a Merry Christmas,  We wish you a Merry Christmas,  We wish you a Merry Christmas   and a Happy New Year
```

Here's a new Time Signature: 3/4 Time. Just means that there are 3 beats per bar, not 4.

Entire C Chord Family Plus 5 of 5: Morning Has.....

C / 1	Dm / 2m	G / 5	F / 4
3 2 3	0	5 0 2	3 2 0

1 + 2 + 3 + | 1 + 2 + 3 + | 1 + 2 + 3 + | 1 + 2 + 3 +
bro - ken, | like the first | morn -

C		Em / 3m	Am / 6m
3 3	3 0	2 0	0 2 4

1 + 2 + 3 + | 1 + 2 + 3 + | 1 + 2 + 3 + | 1 + 2 + 3 +
ing, | black - bird has | spok - | en

D / 5 of 5	G / 5	G7	C
0 2 4	5	3 0 2	3 0 2

1 + 2 + 3 + | 1 + 2 + 3 + | 1 + 2 + 3 + | 1 + 2 + 3 +
Like the first | bird, | | praise for the

F		C	Am
3 2	5 2 3	3 2	0 2 3

1 + 2 + 3 + | 1 + 2 + 3 + | 1 + 2 + 3 + | 1 + 2 + 3 +
sing - ing, | | praise for the | morn -

D	G	C	F
0 2	0 2 3	3 0 2	3 0

1 + 2 + 3 + | 1 + 2 + 3 + | 1 + 2 + 3 + | 1 + 2 + 3 +
ing, | praise for them | spring - | ing

G	C	F	C
2 0 2	3 0 2	3 0 2 4	5 3

1 + 2 + 3 + | 1 + 2 + 3 + | 1 + 2 + 3 + | 1 + 2 + 3 +
fresh from the | world

87654325

The basslines of enough songs employ the **87654325** model to justify one page anyway. It's primarily a Major Scale in reverse, but what's interesting is that several of the chords in the progression are *not* represented by the **Root Note**, rather by the **3rd**. This is most irregular: The bassist almost always plays the **Root** on **Count 1** of every measure.

But it works because, well, everyone loves the Major Scale, I guess!
First I'll show you the progression with the **Triad Roots** for all the chords and then how the same sequence is smoothed out by switching to the **3rds**:

| G / 1 | D / 5 | Em / 6m | D / 5 | C / 4 | G / 1 | Am / 2m | D / 5 |

```
|-5-----------------|-2-----------------|-------------------|-------------------|
|-----5-------------|-------5-----------|-----3-------------|-------5-----------|
|-------------------|-------------------|-----------3-------|-5-----------------|
|-------------------|-------------------|-------------------|-------------------|
  1 + 2 + 3 + 4 +     1 + 2 + 3 + 4 +     1 + 2 + 3 + 4 +     1 + 2 + 3 + 4 +
```

```
|-5----(4)----------|-2-----------------|-------------------|-------------------|
|-------------------|-------5-----------|-----3-----(2)-----|-------5-----------|
|-------------------|-------------------|-------------------|-5-----------------|
|-------------------|-------------------|-------------------|-------------------|
  1 + 2 + 3 + 4 +     1 + 2 + 3 + 4 +     1 + 2 + 3 + 4 +     1 + 2 + 3 + 4 +
```
Your Smiling Face (James Taylor)

And here are some variants. They all start the same but end differently:

| C / 1 | G / 5 | Am / 6m | C / 1 | F / 4 | Dm / 2m | G / 5 |

```
|-5---4-----3-------|-------------------|-----3-------------|-----5-----5-------|
|-------------------|-------5-----------|-----------5-------|-------------------|
|-------------------|-------------------|-------------------|-------------------|
  1 + 2 + 3 + 4 +     1 + 2 + 3 + 4 +     1 + 2 + 3 + 4 +     1 + 2 + 3 + 4 +
```
Penny Lane (Beatles)

| E / 1 | B / 5 | C#m / 6m | B / 5 | A / 4 | B / 5 |

```
|-7-----6-----------|-4-----------------|-----7-------------|-7-------4---6-----|
|-------------------|-------7-----------|-5-----------------|-------------------|
|-------------------|-------------------|-------------------|-------------------|
  1 + 2 + 3 + 4 +     1 + 2 + 3 + 4 +     1 + 2 + 3 + 4 +     1 + 2 + 3 + 4 +
```
All I Have To Do Is Dream (Nitty Gritty Dirt Band)

| A / 1 | E / 5 | F#m / 6m | E / 5 | D / 4 | E / 5 | A / 1 |

```
|-7-7---7-6---6-4---|-4-----------------|-4-4---4-----------|-0-----------------|
|-------------------|-----7-----7-7-----|-----------7---7---|-------------------|
|-------------------|-------------------|-------------------|-------------------|
  1 + 2 + 3 + 4 +     1 + 2 + 3 + 4 +     1 + 2 + 3 + 4 +     1 + 2 + 3 + 4 +
```
Tears in Heaven (Eric Clapton)

The Flatted Seventh Degree

Without the Flatted Seventh, there would be no such thing as The Blues.
We would all be happy all the time, and not so self-absorbed.
Curse you, Flatted Seventh!

So true. But then life would be dull, so let's embrace our new bummed out friend.

But why go and flat the **7th** in the first place? What's wrong with a rounded **7th**?

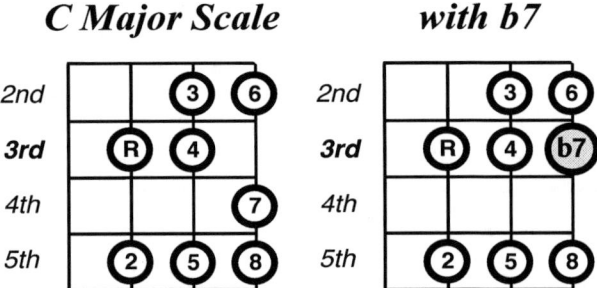

In the **C Major Scale**, all the notes are natural, so the 7th note is C - D - E - F - G - A - **B**. If you flat it, you get **Bb**. Compare the two scales to the right:

The scale with the **b7th** sounds darker, not exactly Minor, but.....bluesier.

It's not a Do-Re-Mi Major Scale, but it's a *kind* of Major Scale because it still contains a **Major 3rd degree**. It has a name: the **Mixolydian Scale**, one of the "Greek Modes."

The **C Mixolydian Scale** actually comes from the **Key of F**. We haven't said much about the **Key of F**, but if you take a look at the Circle of Fifths and go down a **5th** from **C** at the 12 o'clock position, you find **F** at 11 o'clock.

The **F Major Scale** is the following: **F - G - A - Bb - C - D - E - F**. You know how we generate the chords in the Chord Family; each note becomes a Triad **Root Note**, and we count **1 - 3 - 5** from there.

Well, instead of picking off just the Triad, *we can run the entire scale from each note*. That's what a **mode** is. In the **Key of F**, we run the **F Major Scale** from each degree, and each of those scales is called a different mode, although they *all* contain *all* the same notes: **F - G - A - Bb - C - D - E - F**.

From **C** note to **C** note in the **F Major Scale**, it's: **C - D - E - F- G - A - Bb - C**, ***and the Bb note is the 7th degree*** in what is called the **C Mixolydian Mode**. (The other modes don't really concern us now, but they have names like Dorian and Lydian. And Phrygian and Locrian and Aeolian.)

From the perspective of the **C Major Scale**, where the **7th** is a *natural* **B** note, it's convenient to call the **Bb** a Flatted Seventh, but now you know the real story. We'll come back to this issue when we talk about Seventh chords, but first we should examine the individual **b7th** notes in the scale, whatever scale it is.

The Box Pattern and the b7th

There is a pattern of 4 notes that bassists like to call **The Box Pattern** that includes the **Root**, the **5th**, the **b7th** and the **Octave**. Here it is, both down and up the neck:

This down-the-neck version has its **Root** on the **A/3rd** string, so it's in the **Key of A**. I've always thought of a *box pattern* as being composed of any groups of notes on the neck that are within easy reach of each other, but many bassists consider this *particular* set of notes as *The* Box Pattern.

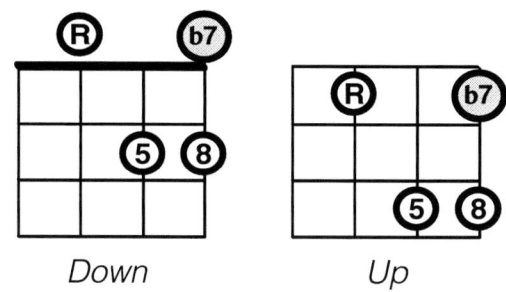

Down   Up

Fun: Even up the neck, the notes are all located within 3 frets of each other, and you can use any combination of 1st and 3rd/4th fingers to play it.

Now that we're getting away from that happy-happy Major Scale sound and starting to inject a more sinister, bluesier sound, let's revisit the **Twelve Bar Blues** progression:

(1) The first 4 bars are dominated by the **1 chord**, with maybe some **4 chord** thrown in.
(2) The second 4 bars start off with the friendly **4 chord**, but then return to the **1 chord**.
(3) The last 4 bars start with the more exciting **5 chord**, and may or may not pass through the **4 chord** on the way to the **1 chord**. The last bar might be occupied by the **5 chord**, in which case it would be called the Blues Turnaround, as it points you toward home.

Many of the following riffs can be inserted into the Twelve Bar Blues progression. Let's start with a riff that goes through all 4 notes in order, and adds a little syncopation. It's in the **Key of G**, and this version of the Twelve Bar Blues has the minimal number of chord changes:

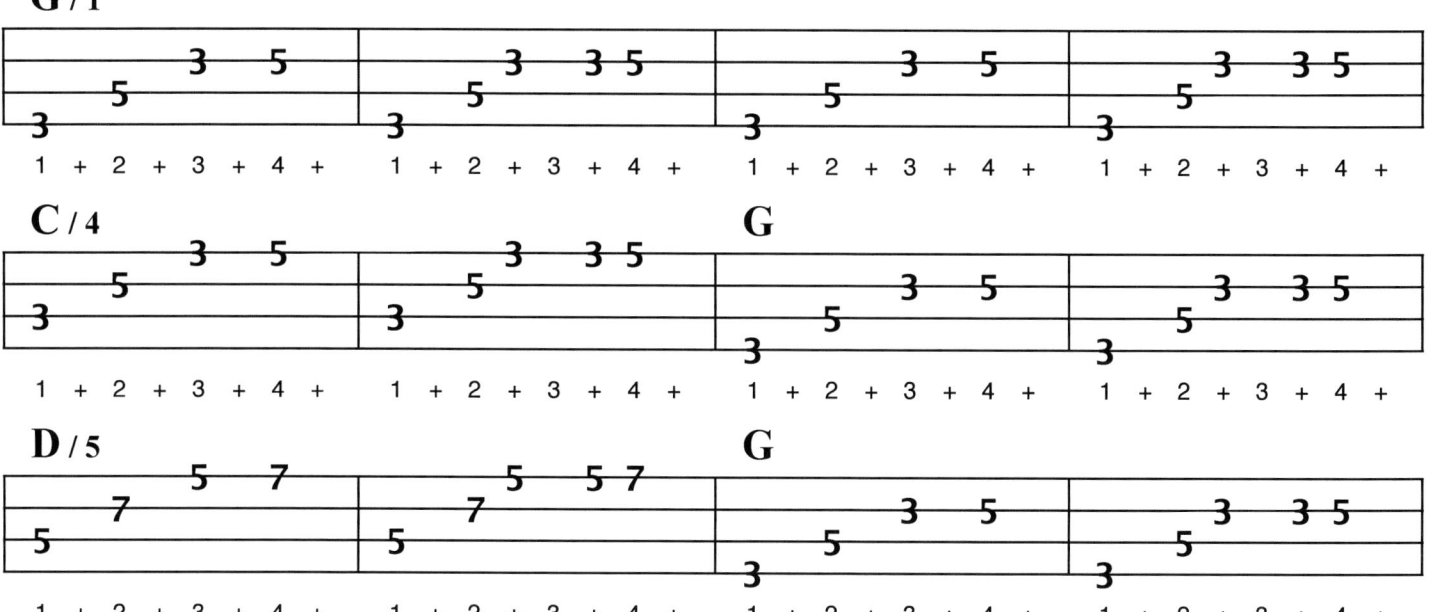

68   This version, in the **Key of A**, also contains all 4 notes, mostly in reverse order, and uses a busier **1 - 4 - 5** progression, with almost a *maximal* number of changes:

A / 1   **D / 4**   **A**

```
|--------7-7-5-5---------|------------7-7-5-5---7-7---|--------7-7-5-5---------|--------7-7-5-5---------|
|--------------------7-7-|----5-5---------------------|----5-5-----------7-7---|----5-5-----------7-7---|
|-5-5--------------------|----------------------------|------------------------|------------------------|
|------------------------|----------------------------|------------------------|------------------------|
  1 + 2 + 3 + 4 +            1 + 2 + 3 + 4 +             1 + 2 + 3 + 4 +          1 + 2 + 3 + 4 +
```

D   **A**

```
|--------7-7-5-5---------|--------7-7-5-5---------|--------7-7-5-5---------|--------7-7-5-5---------|
|------------------7-7---|------------------7-7---|----5-5-----------7-7---|----5-5-----------7-7---|
|-5-5--------------------|-5-5--------------------|------------------------|------------------------|
  1 + 2 + 3 + 4 +           1 + 2 + 3 + 4 +           1 + 2 + 3 + 4 +          1 + 2 + 3 + 4 +
```

E / 5   **D**   **A**   **D**   **A**   **E**

```
|--------9-9-7-7---------|--------7-7-5-5---------|--------------7-7-------|--------------7-7-----9-9-|
|------------------9-9---|------------------7-7---|----7-7-----------------|----7-7-----------7-7-----|
|-7-7--------------------|----5-5-----------------|--------5-5-------------|--------5-5---------------|
|------------------------|------------------------|-5-5--------------------|-5-5----------------------|
  1 + 2 + 3 + 4 +           1 + 2 + 3 + 4 +          1 + 2 + 3 + 4 +          1 + 2 + 3 + 4 +
```

It's amazing what you can do with just the **8th** and the **♭7th** degrees.
Here is a **5th of the 5th** deal in the **Key of G**:

G / 1

```
|-5-5-3-5-----------3---|-5-5-3-5-----------3---|-5-5-3-5-----------3---|-5-5-3-5-----------5---|
  1 + 2 + 3 + 4 +         1 + 2 + 3 + 4 +         1 + 2 + 3 + 4 +         1 + 2 + 3 + 4 +
```

A / 5 of 5   **D / 5**

```
|-7-7-5-7-----------5---|-7-7-5-7---------------|-------------5-|-7-7-5-7-----------5---|-7-7-5-7---|
                                                  1 + 2 + 3 + 4+                                     
  1 + 2 + 3 + 4 +         1 + 2 + 3 + 4 +         1 + 2 + 3 + 4 +         1 + 2 + 3 + 4 +
                                 You Really Got Me (The Kinks)
```

Rather sparse, in the **Key of F**. Got the **Root**, **♭7th** and **8th**:

F / 1

```
|------------3-1---|------3-----------|------------------|------------3-1---|------------------|
|-1----------------|------------------|------------------|-1----------------|------------------|
  1 + 2 + 3 + 4 +    1 + 2 + 3 + 4 +    1 + 2 + 3 + 4 +    1 + 2 + 3 + 4 +
         Pick Up the Pieces (Average White Band)
```

Two shorties in the open **Key of A** that manage to use all four Box Pattern notes. With slurs:

```
|------2-----0-----|------2-----0-----|    2ᴾ 0           2ᴾ 0
|--------0ᴴ2-------|--------0ᴴ2-------|   ⌢              ⌢
|-0----------------|-0----------------|   ---------2----   ---------2----
                                           -0------------   -0------------
  1 + 2 + 3 + 4 +    1 + 2 + 3 + 4 +    1 + 2 + 3 + 4 +    1 + 2 + 3 + 4 +
```

There's another class of Box Pattern riffs that "hang high": They start at the Octave and dip down to the **b7ths** and **5ths**. These are all in the **Key of A**, all mid-neck, all on the **1 chord**:

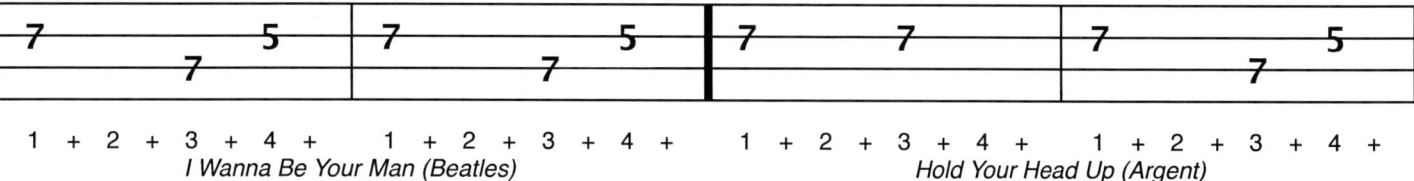
I Wanna Be Your Man (Beatles)   Hold Your Head Up (Argent)

These two have chromatic Passing Tones:

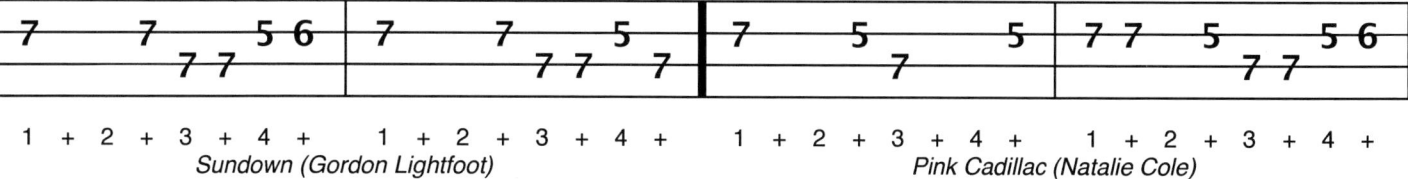
Sundown (Gordon Lightfoot)   Pink Cadillac (Natalie Cole)

These two are syncopated, the second more than the first (synced notes are syrcled):

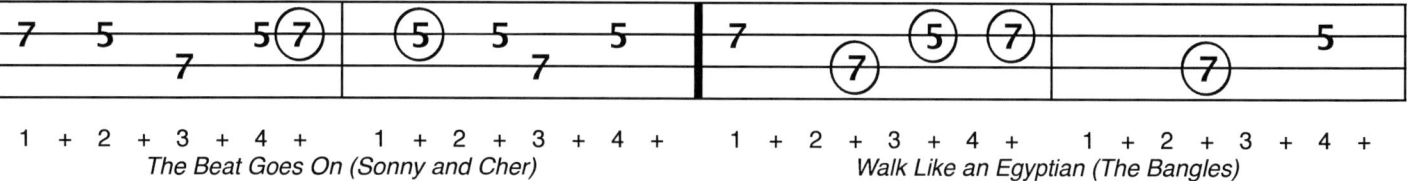
The Beat Goes On (Sonny and Cher)   Walk Like an Egyptian (The Bangles)

This one's just cool:

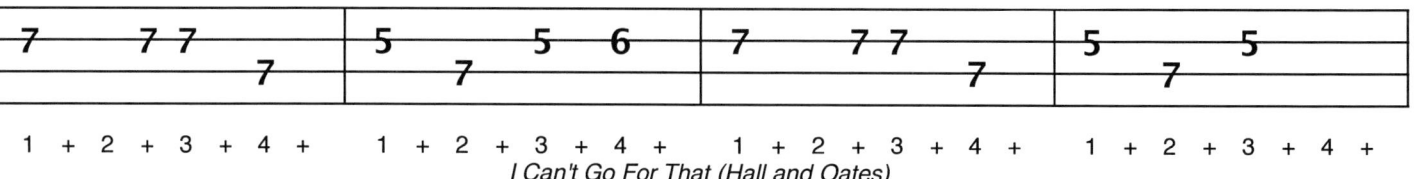
I Can't Go For That (Hall and Oates)

There's no reason you can't reach down into the lower octave.
The **7 - 5 - 7** notes are one octave lower than the **0 - 3 - 5**:

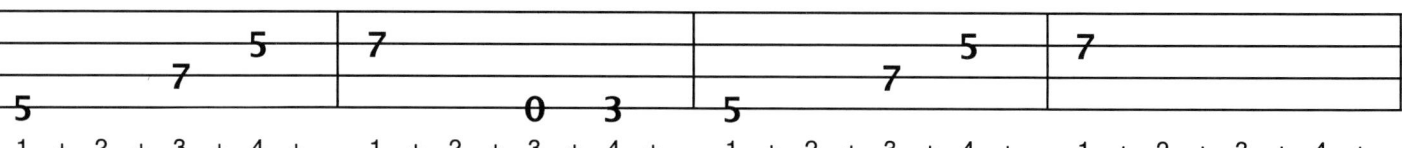

Let's add another scale degree, **the 4th (D)** to **Count 4**. Sounds pretty good:

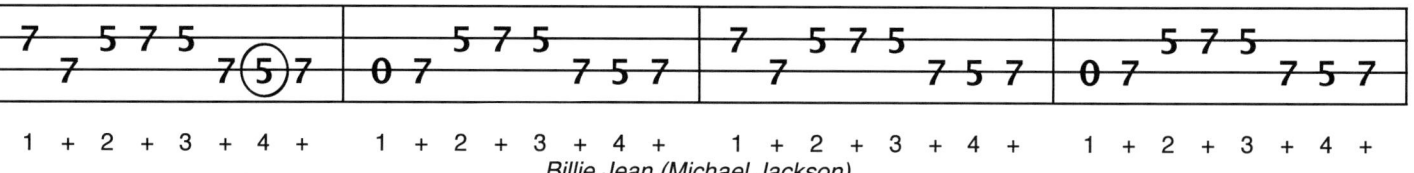
Billie Jean (Michael Jackson)

Swing Time

We're about to return to the boogie-woogie pattern, and then delve deeper into the blues, so this is a good time to discuss **swing time**. This is a case where a sound bite is worth a thousand words, so listen to the audio track on this. But it has to do with the underlying rhythmic structure of music, *and how the notes **within the beat** relate to each other*.

So we're talking about Eighth-notes. In all the playing we've done to this point, each *count* of music, represented by the Quarter-note, is divided exactly in half into two Eighth-notes, so we get an even "rat-tat-tat-tat-tat" sound playing Eight to the Bar.

But many blues and rock and roll have an underlying rhythm that is *uneven*, a sort of asymmetrical, limping quality, sort of a "1.....uh 2.....uh 3.....uh 4" sound.

In poetry, this rhythm is known as **iambic meter**. Sir Walter Scott's poem "The Lady of the Lake" contains this line: "The stag at eve had drunk his fill." Think of the words *stag*, *eve*, *drunk* and *fill* as **Counts 1**, **2**, **3** and **4** of a measure and the other words as the "**and**" counts.

Arithmetically what we are doing is splitting each beat into three "sub-beats" called **triplets (1 + a)** instead of **duplets (1 +)**, *and then playing on only the **1st** and **3rd*** sub-beats. That is, we play notes in the 1st and 3rd *slots*. So if we take the Eighth-note Box Pattern example from several pages back and apply it to the iambic meter, we get the following:

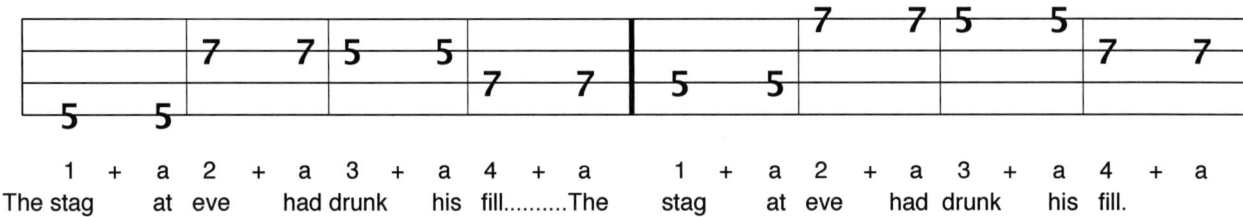

You can hear what I mean about limping; the bad leg comes a bit late in each stride, but the good leg keeps landing on time. Another way to see it is that the second note in each beat is lightly delayed, but the overall pulse and tempo stay the same.

So the first note occupies 2/3 of the beat and the second note occupies 1/3 of it. *But sometimes we play **on all three** of the triplet sub-beats*. This compares to the meter for one of Sir Walter Scott's later works, "There *Was* a Drunk *Stag* from Nan*tuck*et." In practice, we don't habitually fill in that second sub-beat; it's just for an accent:

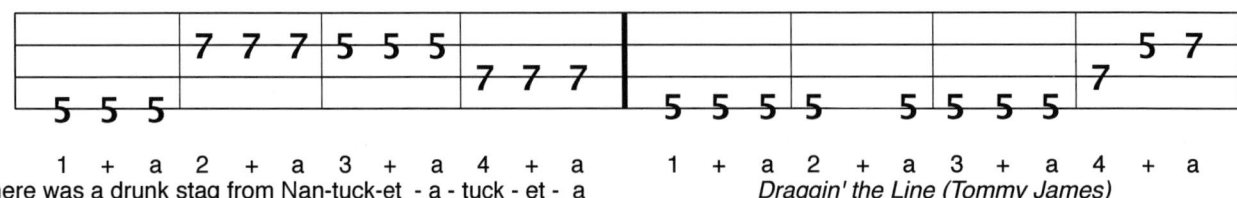

Boogie Back With a ♭7th

Now that you've met the **♭7th** degree, it's time to revisit the boogie-woogie. On the left, you see the **R - 3 - 5 - 6 - 8** version, and on the right we switch in **♭7th** degree for the **8th**:

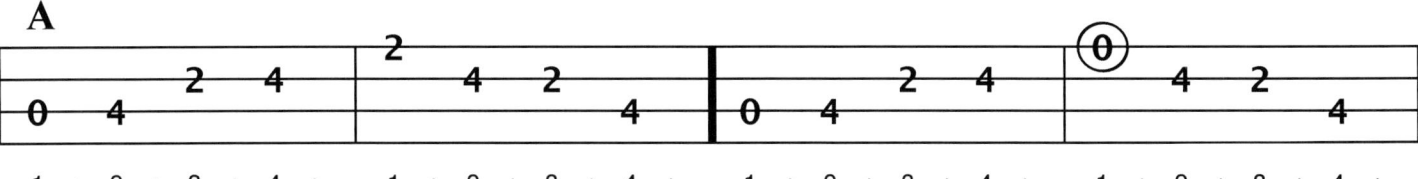

The **♭7th** makes everything it touches sound just a bit more bluesy, yeah?
Often, people will alternate the two patterns above randomly. The whatevs.
Let's do a pass through the Twelve Bar Blues progression using the **♭7th**.
And why not try it in *swing time*? To save space, I'll write it out in
Straight **Eighth**-notes, but now you *know* how to *swing* it:

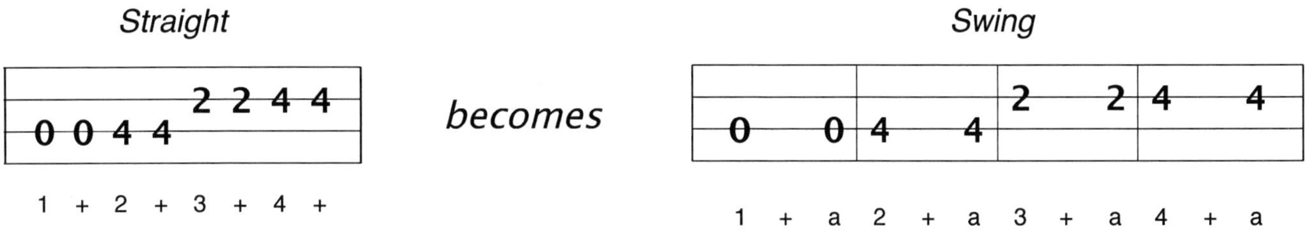

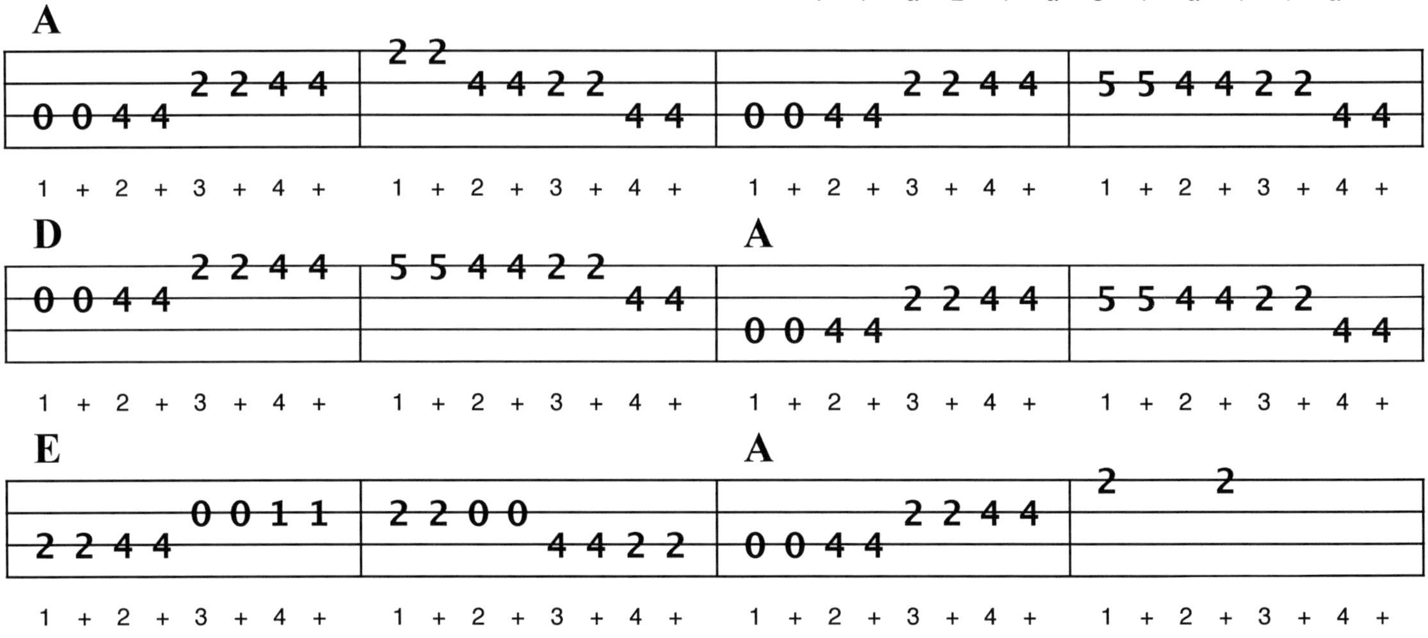

Here's a Circle of Fifths ending you sometimes hear, with chromatic approach notes.
You can substitute it for the last two bars (*Amp Fling Bruce Emery's Amp*):

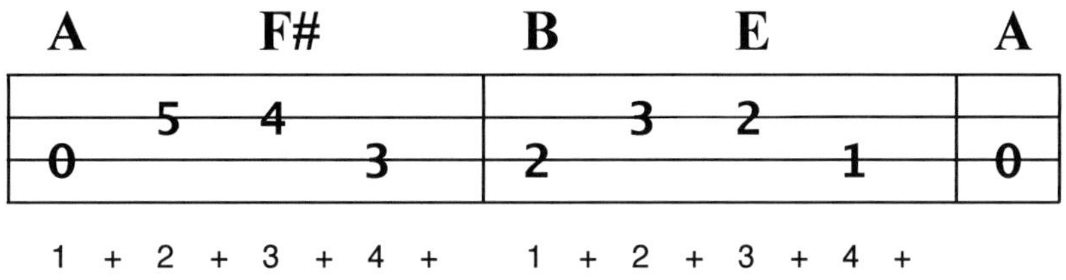

The Movable Boogie Pattern

Of course, everything we just did in the Open Position of the **Key of A** can be shifted to the Open Position in the **Key of E** by going down one string. But if you're going to play it in any other key, you will need a *movable pattern*.

So we'll stay in the **Key of A**, but move to the *fretted unison locations of the same notes,* down one string and up five frets. Okay to slide the 4th finger to the 9th fret on **Count 2**:

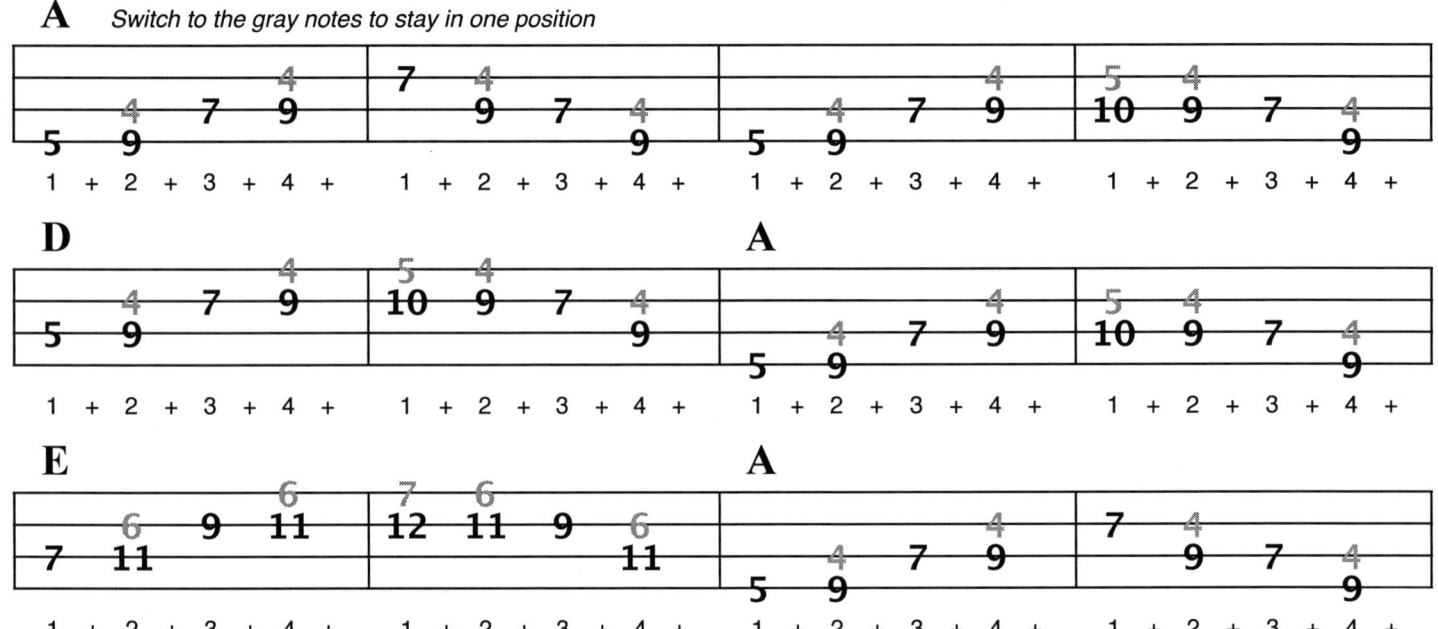

Now you can just track down the **Root Note** for any key you need using the familiar Fretboard Diagram to the right. And here are the first 4 bars of three more boogie patterns up the neck, still in the **Key of A**. You can move them for the **D** and **E** chords:

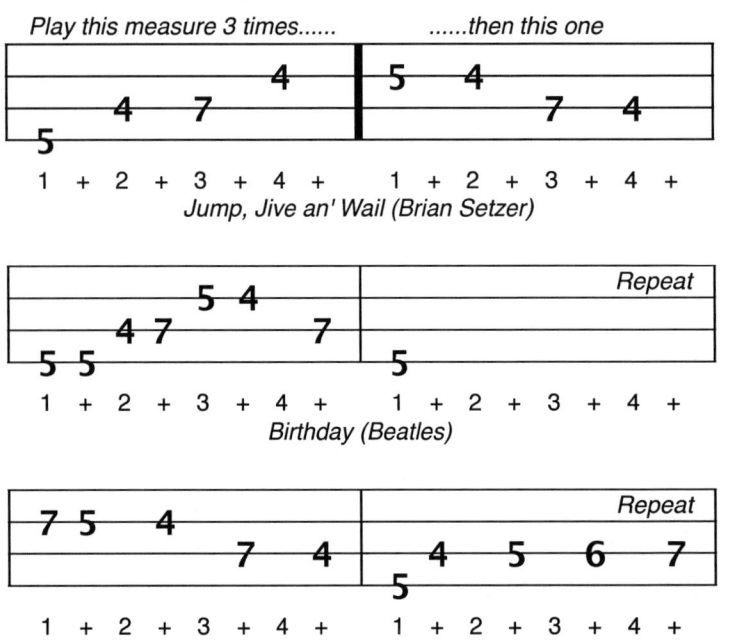

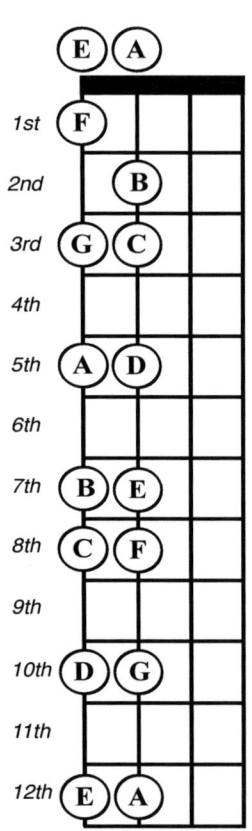

*You **won't** find any **♭7ths** on this page of boogie riffs.*

Here's the first line to a fancy riff that includes the swing rhythm,
a descending line, two syncopated chord changes and some chromatics:

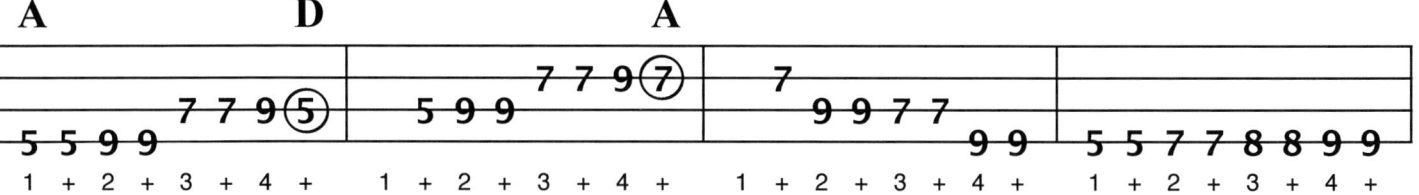

Another bluesy thing you can do is to grab the **Minor 3rd**, or **♭3rd**, from the Blues Scale (coming soon) and use it to slide up one fret into the **Major 3rd**. The blues really tries to straddle the fence between the Major and Minor modalities. Toggles back and forth.

This slide, unlike previous ones, has a *specific* starting point;
you actually want to hear the note at the fret where it originates.

Back to Open Position, still in **A**. These two riffs are beaten Eight to the Bar:

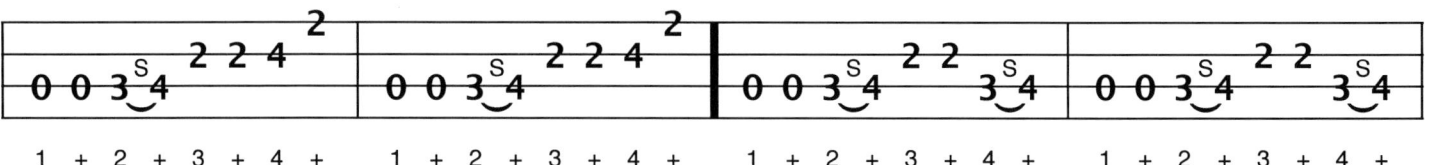

This one's swingy and a little sparser:

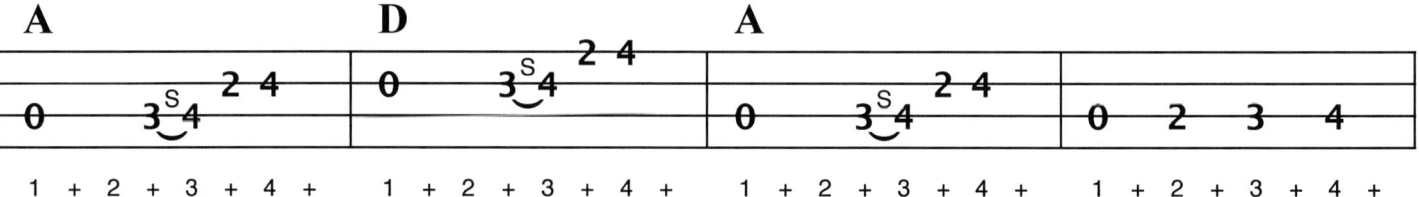

The last example is what happens when you cross the boogie-woogie with the Jazz Turnaround:

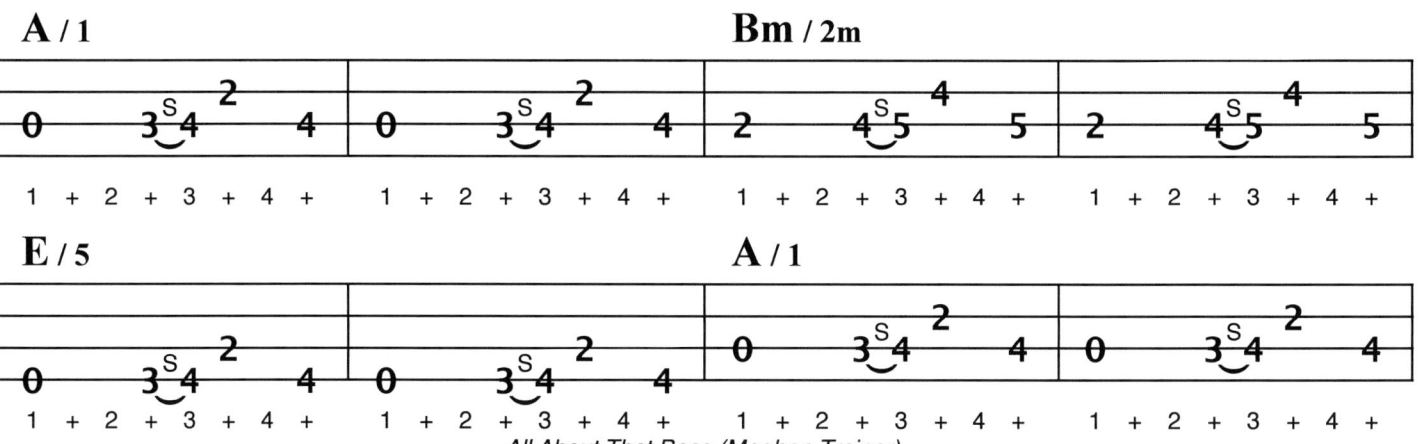

All About That Bass (Meghan Trainor)

The Blues and Blues-Based Rock

The Blues is a hodgepodge of European and African musical influences, and I suppose there are hundreds (thousands?) of books that describe the history and the personalities. All *I* want to do is show you how to find your way around the chords and the scales.

The Chords. Major chords work just fine, the old **1 - 4 - 5** in the Twelve Bar Blues. For the bassist, that could be the end of the story. Seventh chords, of the **b7th** variety, are pretty common as well, but the bassist can leave that whole responsibility to the guitarist and keyboardist. As long as we pay attention to the **Root**, **3rd** and **5th** of the Major Triad, we're off the hook.

But no. Not only are we going to want to play riffs that include our new friend, the **b7th**, but we'll want to welcome in and assimilate a *newer* friend, too, the **b3rd**. Together, they set the stage and provide the ambience for all the Blues you can use. But you know me, I'm going to want to show you how we get there from here.

And we'll start, as we are wont to do, with the **C Major Scale**.

C	D	E	F	G	A	B
1	2	3	4	5	6	7

I'll draw on several things we talked about before. Such as, the Relative Minor chord. Remember how the **6m chord** has that special relationship with the **1 chord**?

For **C**, it's **Am**. Well, not only is there a Rel Min Chord, there is the Rel Min *Scale*. And we'll use the same process to find it as we did with the **C Mixo Scale (Key of F)**. Take the **C Major Scale**, go to the **6th** degree, **A**, and run it from **A** note to **A** note:

A	B	C	D	E	F	G
1	2	3	4	5	6	7

You now have the **A Natural Minor Scale**, also known as the **A Aeolian Mode**. It has no sharps, just like **C Major**. So where does all this "flatted" stuff come into play? Well, compare this **A Minor Scale** with another old friend of ours, the *A Major Scale*:

A	B	(C#)	D	E	(F#)	(G#)
1	2	3	4	5	6	7

A Major has 3 sharps, so if you want to transform *A Major* into *A Minor*, you need to *flat (naturalize)* the **3rd**, **6th** and **7th** degrees of the A Major Scale.

So we call them the **b3rd** and **b7th** only from the *perspective* of **A Major**, which is the **Parallel Major Scale** to **Am**. (Parallel Major and Minor scales have the same **Roots**.)

But what about the *third* sharp, at the **6th** degree? We haven't mentioned that.

*That's because we are less interested in the 7-note A Minor Scale than we are in the 5-note **A Pentatonic Minor Scale**.*

Take the **A Minor Scale** and look at the two *Half-step* intervals **B** to **C** and **E** to **F**. By tradition, the 5-note Pentatonic Scale is wide open, with notes spaced farther apart, *so there should't be an interval as small as a Half-Step*. So one member of each of those pairs must *gooooooo*.

Of the **B/C** pair, we drop the **B** note (**2nd** degree) and keep the **C** note since **C** is the **Minor 3rd** in the scale, and happens to be the note that renders the whole thing Minor! Of the **E/F** pair, **E** is the mighty **5th**. Gotta hang onto that! So the **6th** is eliminated. *So we are left with the Box Pattern plus the b3rd and 4th*:

A	C	D	E	G
1	b3	4	5	b7

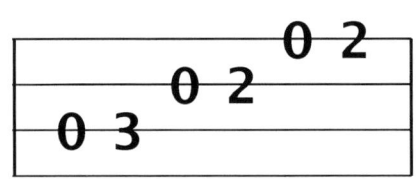 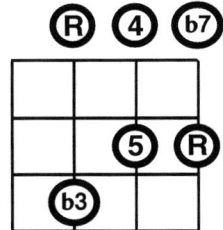

(Of course, those rejected notes [and others] can be invited back in as Passing Tones.) So far, so good. *But why do we care about **the Major perspective**?* Ah. It turns out that we usually play the **A Minor Scale** over/under the *Major* chords in the **A Chord Family**! More evidence that the Blues constantly dithers between Major and Minor modalities.

But what IS the Chord Family here? A nice selection of Majors, Minors and Dims? Nope. Here in Pentatonicville, **all 5 chords are either Major or Seventh**. It's tradition. There is indeed a category called *Minor Blues*, where the **1** and **4 chords** are Minor and the **5 chord** is a Seventh chord. And we'll look at songs in 7-note Minor keys later. But Major-key blues is more popular. Go ahead and run around the scale a bit. I'll wait.....

That kind of poking around in the scale is fun, and I encourage you to experiment. But just remember that a bassline can be too busy in the presence of other instruments. Often, all that's required is a nice, steady **Root Note**, with some flourishes advisable every now and then, say, at the end of a phrase or section of music:

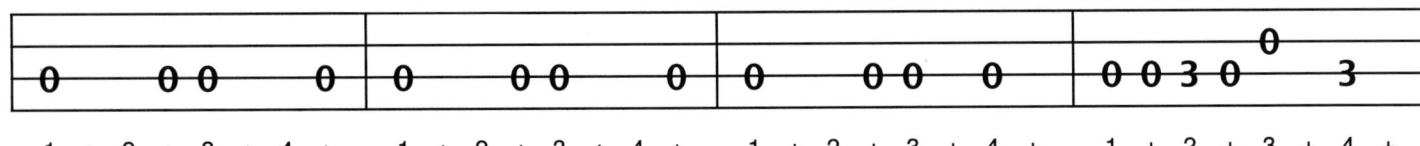

Here are four alternate endings for the final measure above:

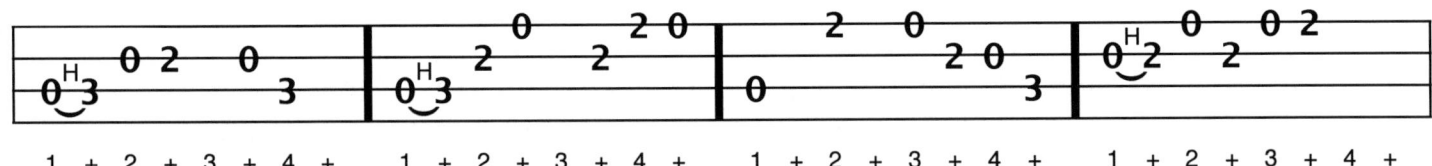

At the other end of the spectrum, the bassist can move at least a little more front and center. Some chromatic notes will be sneaking in, and each of the four examples is a bit more syncopated than the previous one. Keep an eye on those "**and**" Counts:

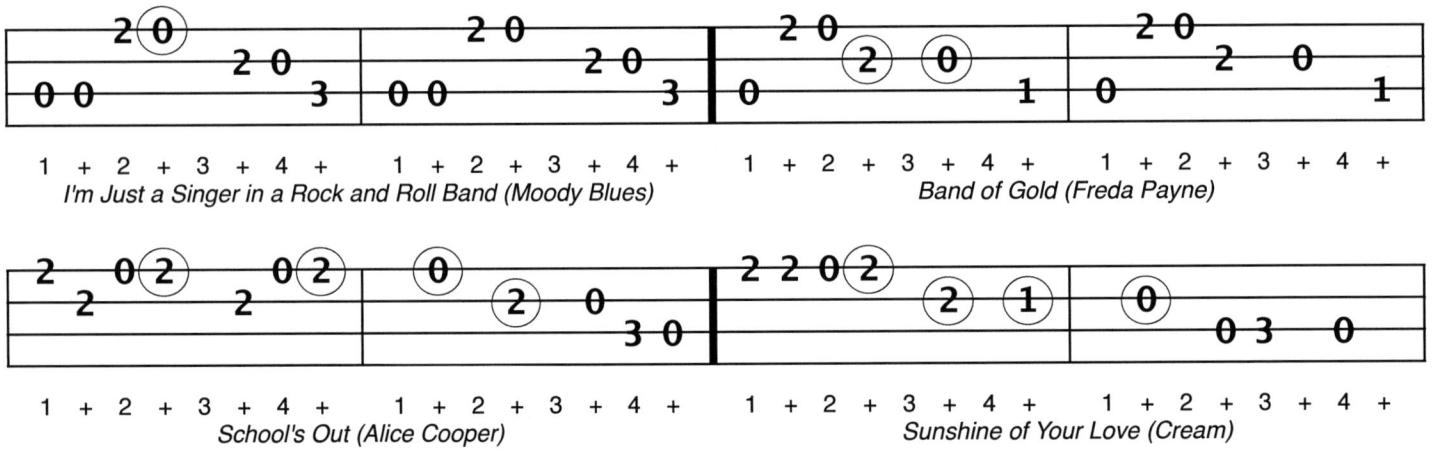

Maybe you realize that I've been holding out on you: *There's another whole string to play!* I've conjured up a bassline to illustrate. Notice that muting is even more important down here. Also notice that, although the **Root** has lower competitors, it retains the gravity and the focus:

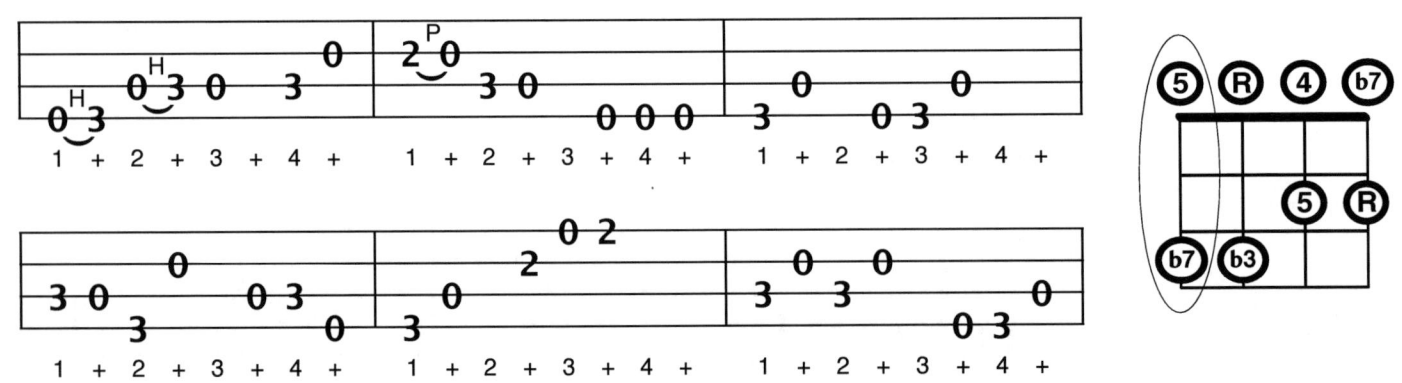

That's not bad, but here's what some of the cool kids have come up with (*swing* this one):

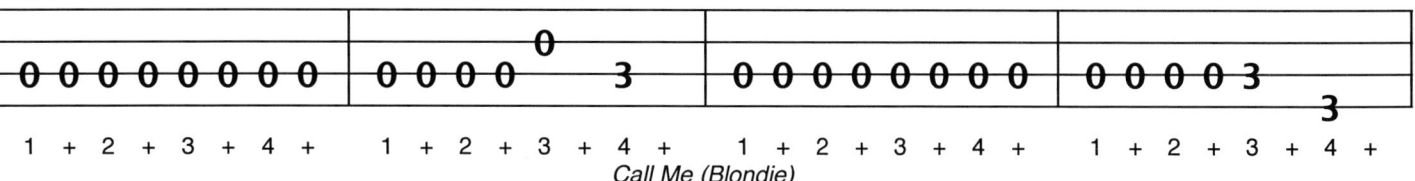
Call Me (Blondie)

Hmm, maybe less is more. Hey, I just came up with that! Less Is More™!

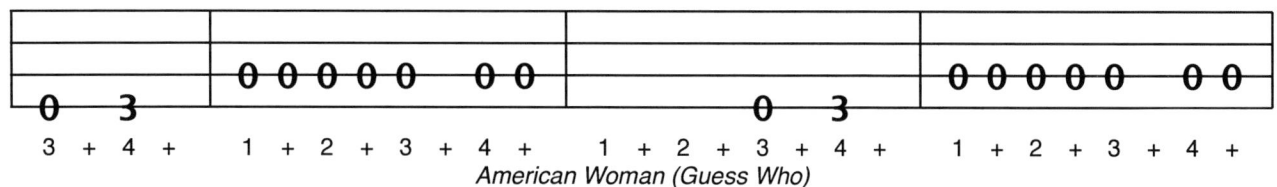
American Woman (Guess Who)

Wow, Lesser Is Even Morer™. Let's see several more down there:

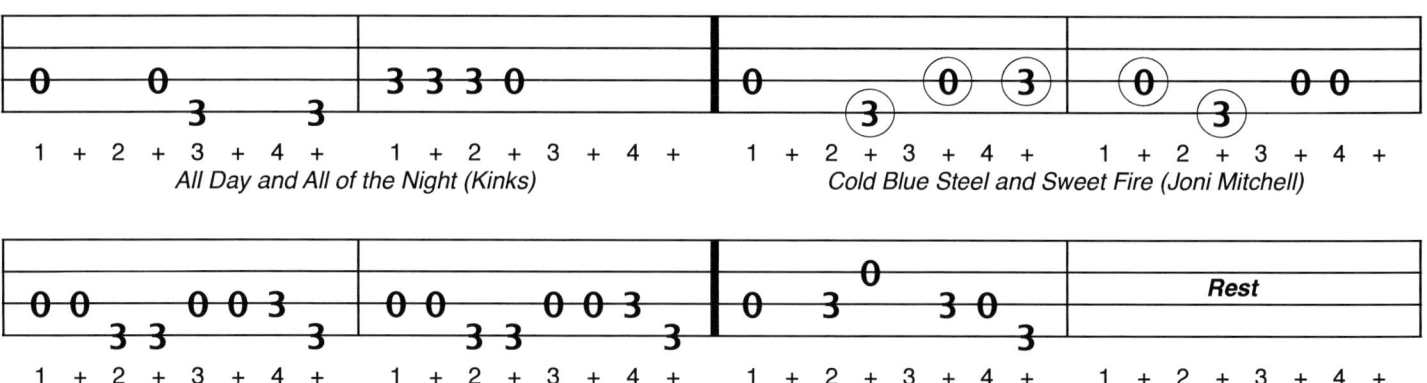
All Day and All of the Night (Kinks)   *Cold Blue Steel and Sweet Fire (Joni Mitchell)*

Fly Robin Fly (Silver Connection)   *Unchain My Heart (Ray Charles)*

Once again, the time has come to take what we've learned Down the Neck and throw it Up the Neck. Find the unison locations of all the notes in the **A Pentatonic Minor Scale**, down one string, up 5 frets. And we might as well add the first few notes from the next higher octave.
Then we can play:

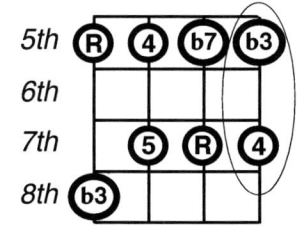

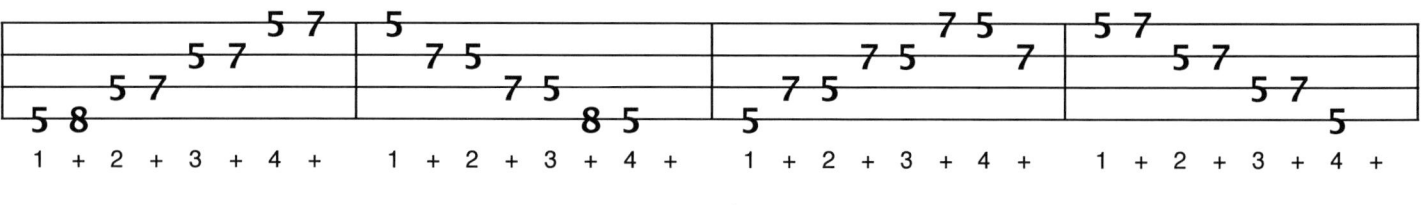

And.....

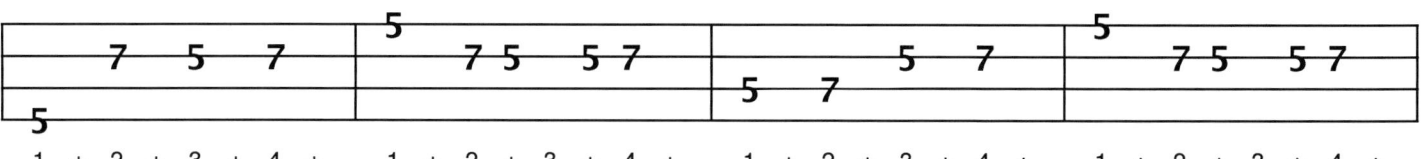
Superstition (Stevie Wonder)

Here's another pathway through the **Am Pentatonic Scale**: Start with the open **E/4th** string, continue in 3rd Position and *slide* up to 5th Position, then reverse course back to the open **E**. Play the whole thing with the 1st and 3rd fingers, sliding up with the 3rd, down with the 1st:

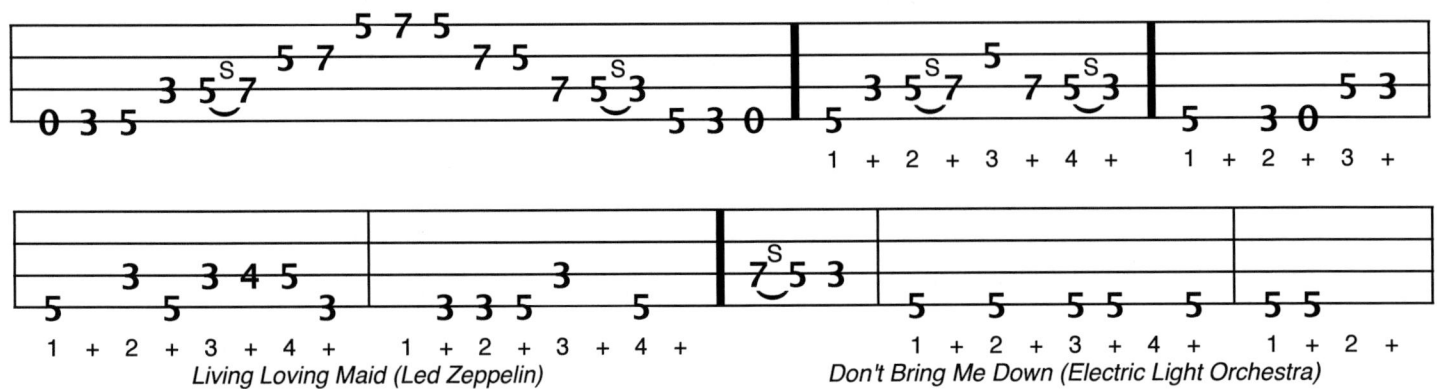

Living Loving Maid (Led Zeppelin)   *Don't Bring Me Down (Electric Light Orchestra)*

Did you notice which note is conspicuous by its absence? It's that "8" from the **E/4th** string! It's a way to avoid that reach from the 5th fret to the 8th fret (not that it's so horrible). Try this:

This is more the way it was done, only in **D**.

It's not just that we're lazy. W'yeah, it is. *Everyone knows* that playing In Position is fabulous, One Finger Per Fret and all. But sometimes it's fun to chillaxicate.

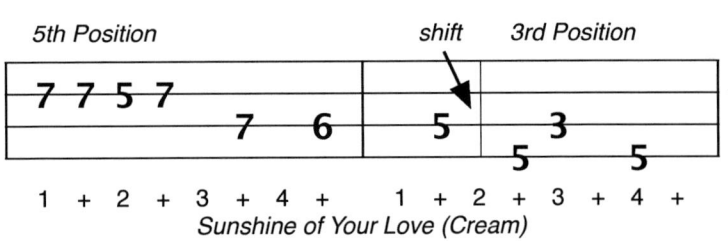

Sunshine of Your Love (Cream)

Let's shift the **Root** back to the **A/3rd** string and play the rest of this page in the **Key of D**. The basic shape is the same, a sort of filled-in Box Pattern, with occasional lower extensions:

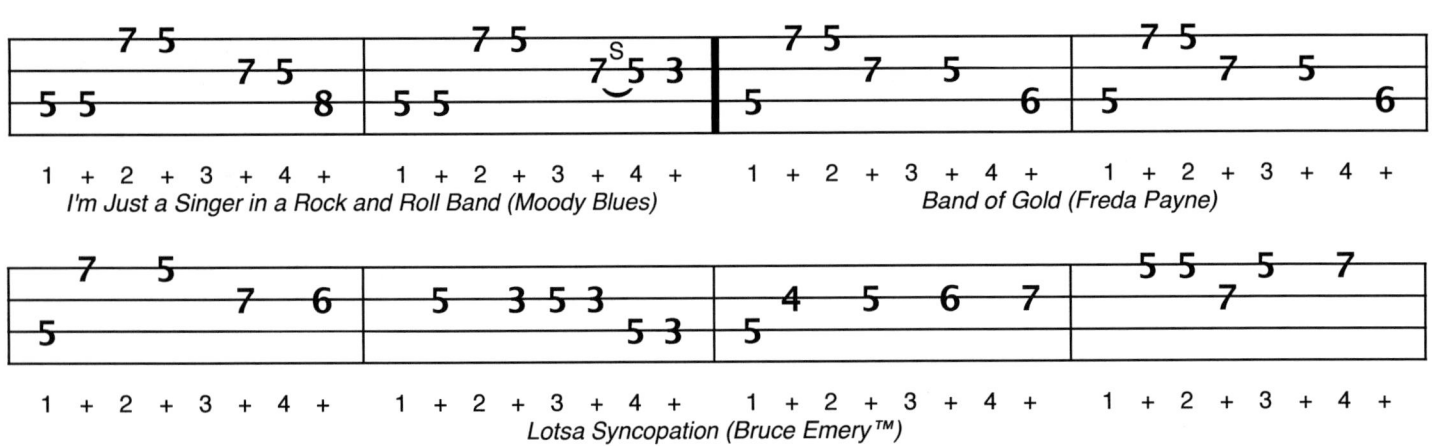

I'm Just a Singer in a Rock and Roll Band (Moody Blues)   *Band of Gold (Freda Payne)*

Lotsa Syncopation (Bruce Emery™)

These next two sort of move around between Open and 5th Positions. Start with the 4th finger:

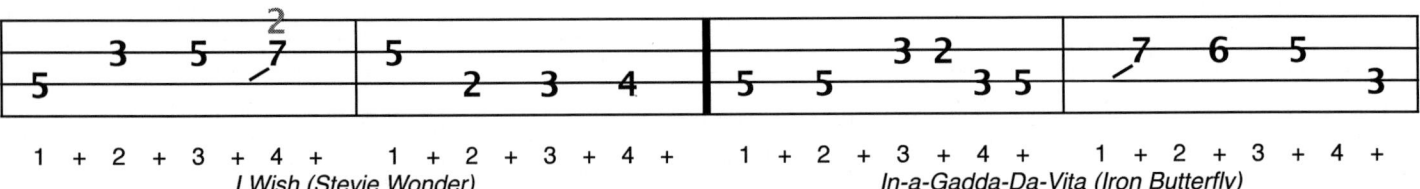

I Wish (Stevie Wonder)   *In-a-Gadda-Da-Vita (Iron Butterfly)*

Chord Changes in Blues Songs

As I alluded to before, the Pentatonic Chord Family contains all Major (or Seventh) chords: **1, b3, 4, 5** and **b7**. Whether the guitarist is playing a Major or a Seventh chord doesn't need to matter to the bassist, just the **Root Notes**.

The **b3rd** degree is of special interest in the blues, foremost as a Passing Tone. The following three basslines in the **Key of E** use the **b3rd** to connect the **1 - 4 - 5**s. Minus the **b3rd**, there would be nothing particularly bluesy about these lines:

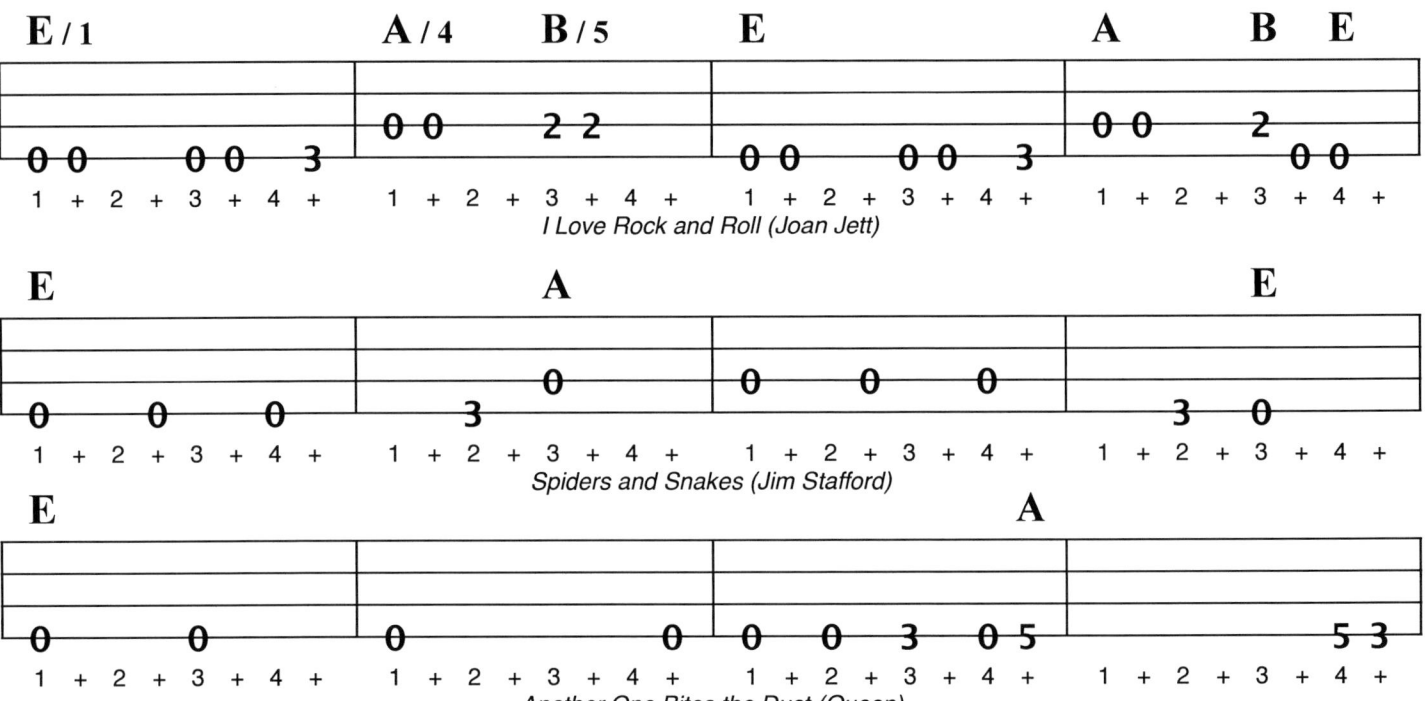

The reason we know these to be changes to actual **4** and **5 chords** is that we dwell on those **Triad Roots** longer. None of our earlier blues riffs exhibited a strong enough *shift in focus* away from the **Key Root** to any other **Triad Root** to qualify as a bona fide chord changes.

Here, the **b3rd** degree gives rise to the *b3 chord* and joins the *b7 chord* in bluesing things up:

The b7 Chord in Popular Music

The **b7 chord** is far and away the most popular blues chord. A favorite chord progression is **1 - b7 - 4**. It doesn't even come close to the **1 - 4 - 5** as the Mainstay of Music, but it sure has gained on it since the 1960s. Here are several examples in their original keys:

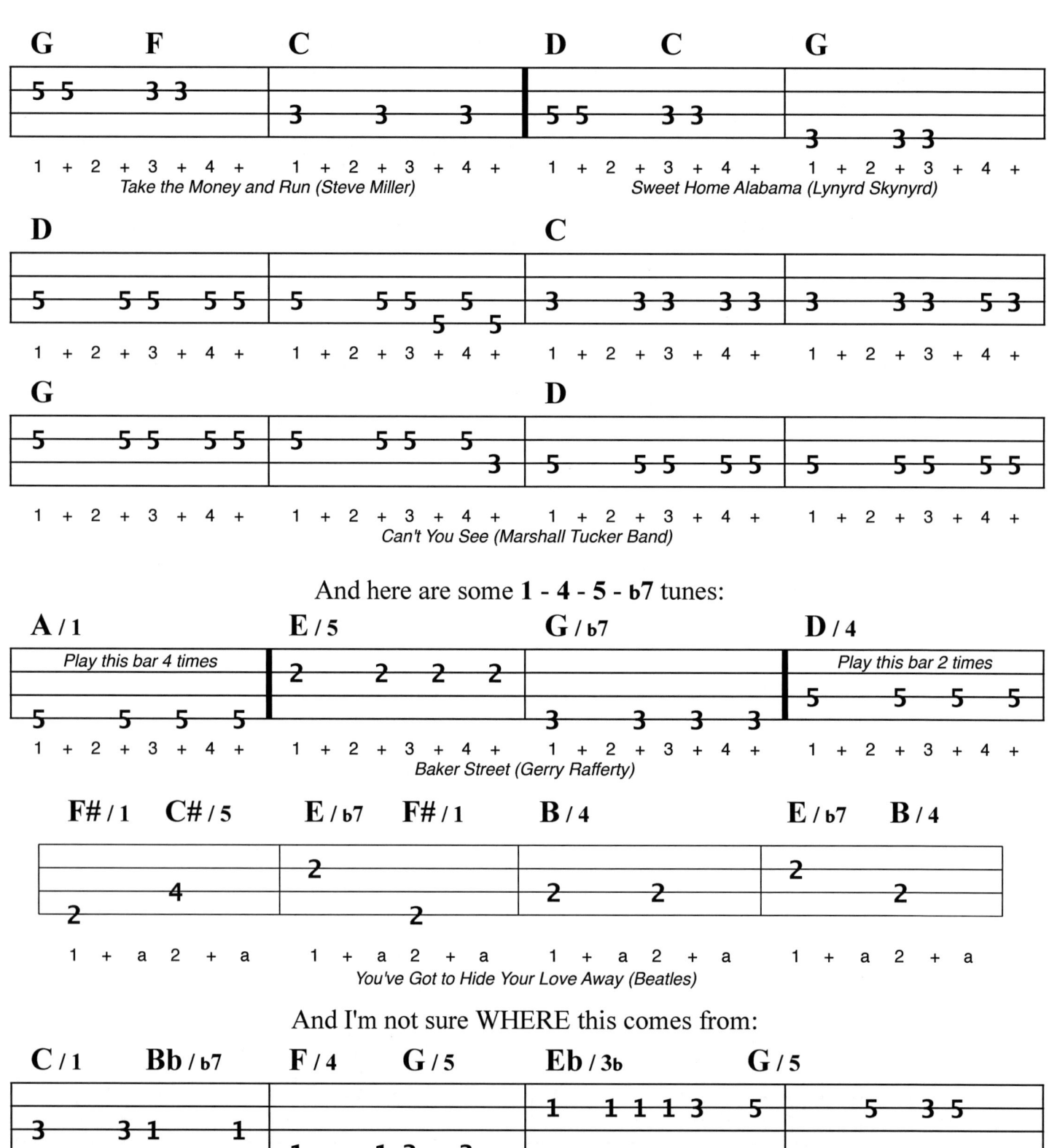

Minor Keys With 7 Notes

Songs in Minor keys are nowhere near as common as songs in Major keys, but here we are!

Let's step back a bit and recall the **A (Natural) Minor Scale**. Remember, we pulled *two* notes out of this scale, the **2nd** and **6th** degrees, to create the **A Pentatonic Minor Scale**. Time to (1) push them back in and (2) generate the Chord Family. How predictable!

We're back to Scale Degree Issues versus Chord Family Issues. The following sequence of letters can be regarded as (1) notes within a scale, or (2) chords within a key. Scale first!

The **A Minor Scale** in Open Position is user friendly, as was its pentatonic counterpart.

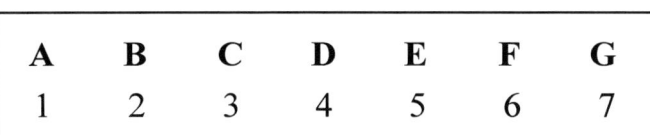 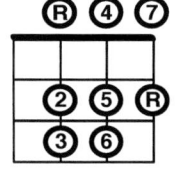 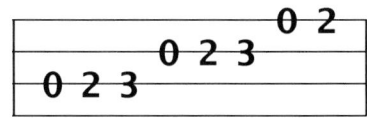

Below and left are the Fretboard Diagram and Tab Diagram for the unison locations for the movable Universal Minor Scale in the **Key of Am**. To the right, it's the **Key of Dm**:

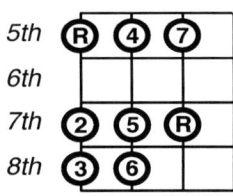 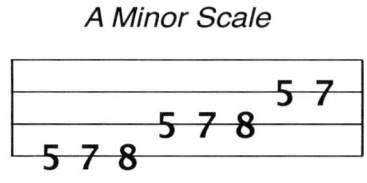 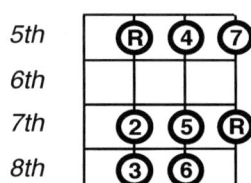 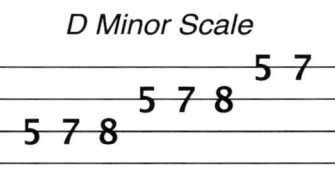

*Notice that now we aren't talking about **flatted** notes. We've gone completely over to the Dark Side and are not comparing these scales to their Parallel Major counterparts.*

It's not so important for you to practice playing these scales as such, but let's do a little of that anyway, shall we? Since it doesn't matter to your fingers, let's use the **Dm Scale**:

That's enough of that. Let's move on to the Chord Family Issues.

The A Minor Chord Family

It should come as no surprise that the **A Minor Chord Family** has essentially the same members as its Relative Major, the **C Chord Family**. *BUT there's a catch*.....

You would assume that all you need to do is to wheel these numbers around so that **A** is in the first slot, **B** is in the second, and so forth.

Am	Bdim	C	Dm	Em	F	G
1	2	3	4	5	6	7

This gives you the array of chords above. So accordingly, the **1 - 4 - 5 chords** are all Minor: **Am**, **Dm** and **Em**. (The other chords, the Major chords? Well, they're just "the other chords." There's no value in calling the **C** chord the **3 chord**, and so on; at least, I've never found any value in it. I just think back to the Relative Major key and recall which chords are in it.)

But here's the problem: That **Em** sounds awfully darned wimpy as the **5 chord**, which is supposedly the ***Dominant*** chord in the family. Doesn't sound very dominating to me. *Or* to musicians down through the centuries, apparently, because a fix has been put in:

*We arbitrarily turn the **Em** chord into an **E Major** chord, even an **E Seventh** chord.*

Now there's a satisfying little *kick* when traveling from the **5** to the **1 chord**. The effect of this Machiavellian maneuver is to force us to go back and modify the scale. It turns the **A Natural Minor** into the **A Harmonic Minor Scale**. Again, if you're curious about some of these theoretical considerations, check out my theory books. All you need to know now about the Harmonic Minor is that the **7th** degree is sharped (**G#** here).

The effect on the bassist is this: Here's a **1 - 4 - 5** progression starting with **Am** and **Dm**. Then you can take your pick of **5 chords**, first **Em**, then **E**. Tell me what you really think:

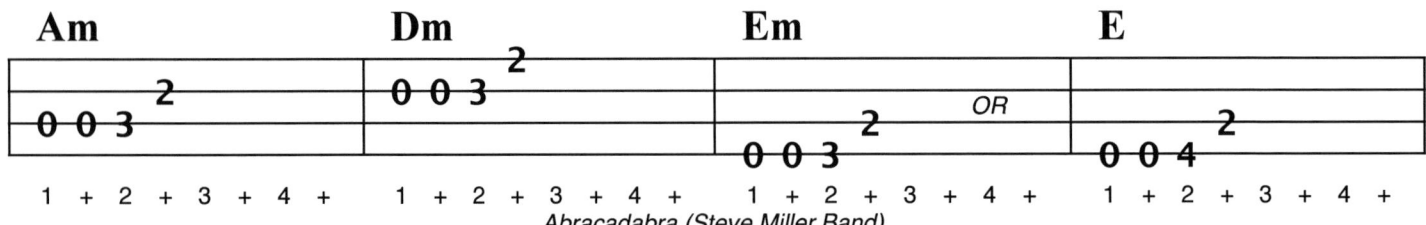
Abracadabra (Steve Miller Band)

Well, Steve picked the Major chord, and you should, too. Actually, it's not required, at all. But most people agree that it's an improvement, that it helps propel the tune along its way.

All you *really* need to do is find the **Root**. Or the **Root** and the **5th**. The problem is the **3rd**, right? If you're gonna mess with Triads, you gotta know whether to play a Major or Minor **3rd**.

"Greensleeves," or "What Child Is This?" deals with this Major/Minor issue by using first the **5 Minor** and then the **5 Major**. How equable:

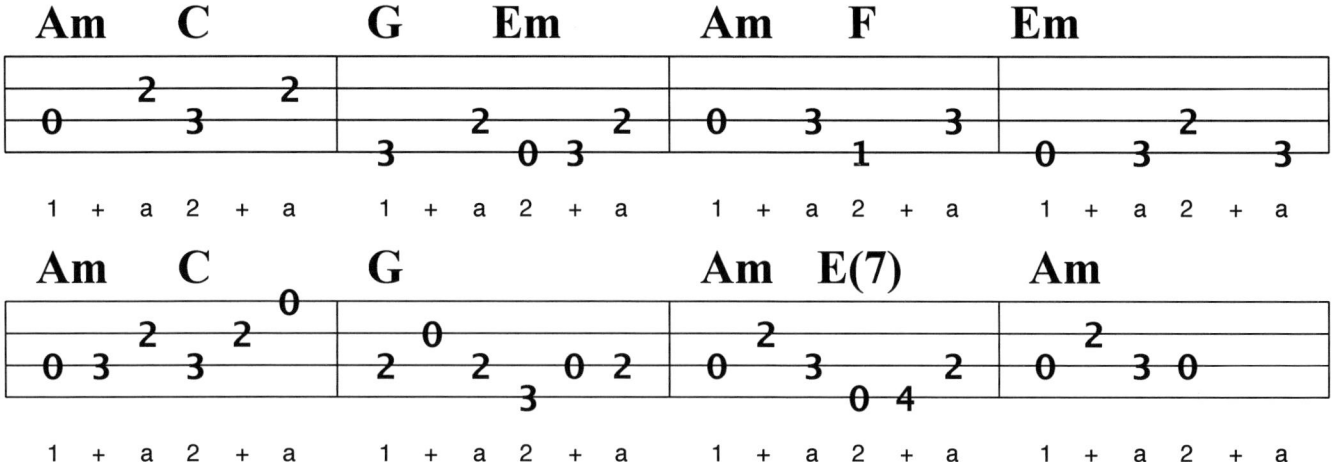

You see what I did in the 6th bar? Started that **G** chord on its *3rd*. Oh *yeah* I did! But this is a great example because it uses (1) all 3 Minor chords, **Am**, **Dm** and **Em**, (2) all 3 Major chords, **C**, **F** and **G** and (3) the **5 chord** as a Major (or Seventh) chord. Here are several more random riffs in **Am**:

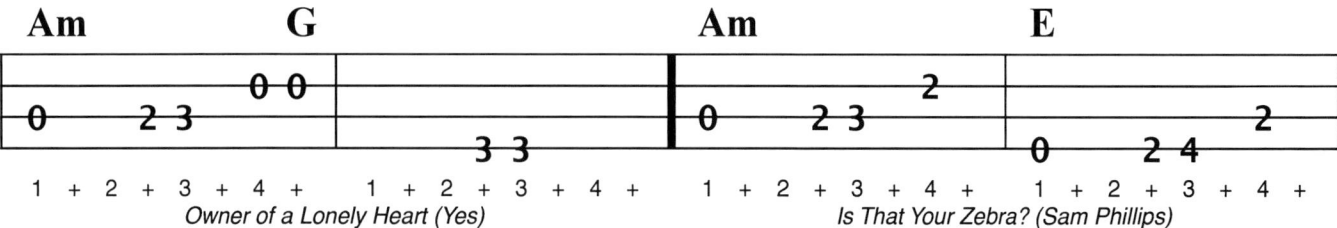

There is a very popular kind of Minor key riff that starts on the **1m chord**, then drops to the **7 chord** a Whole-step below, bottoms out at the **6 chord** another Whole-step down, then turns around and heads back up through the **7 chord** to start over on the **1m** (8 7 6 7 8). The **Key of Bm** is a common choice for this treatment, where the chords are **Bm**, **A** and **G**:

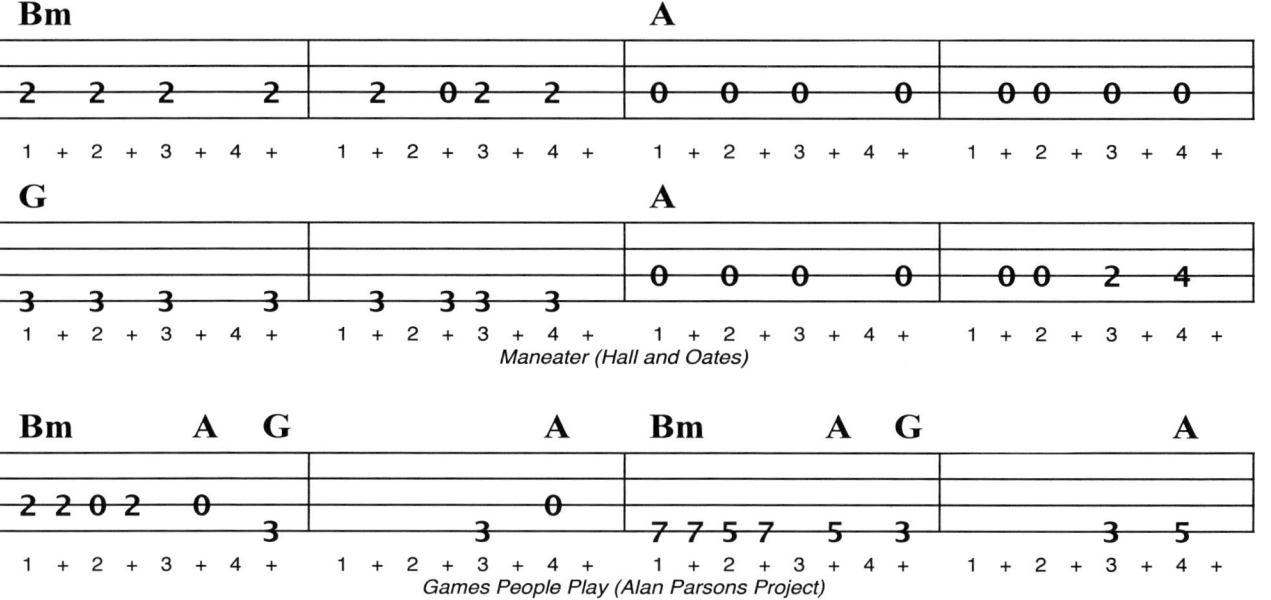

Here's one in the **Key of F#m** (the Relative Minor to the **Key of A**) so **E** and **D** are the next chords down. There are alternating Eighth-notes mixed with plenty of syncopated Quarter-notes. If you find you need to do too much muting, find the unison fretted notes on the next lower string:

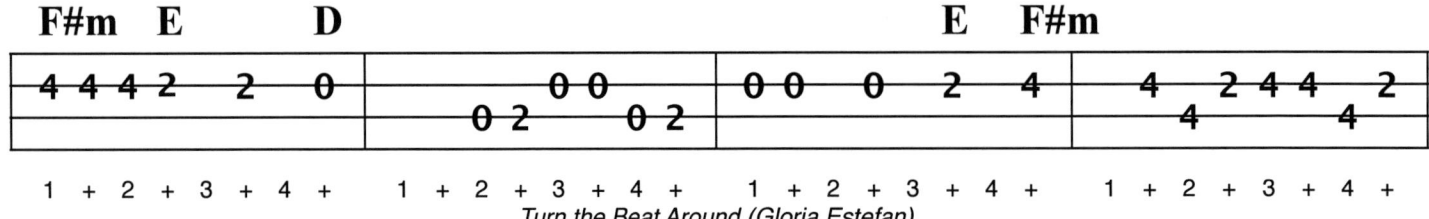
Turn the Beat Around (Gloria Estefan)

The next one is at the other end of the "note density" spectrum. This is in **Key of Dm**, in swing-copated time, with **C** and **Bb** chords:

Layla (Eric Clapton)

"California Dreamin'" was recorded using **Am** guitar chord shapes with a capo placed at the the 4th fret, so the song *sounds* in the **Key of C#m**. I'll present the opening section in the **Key of Am** first, because the Chord Family members are easier to keep track of, then in the **Key of C#m**, because that's what the bass player will need to deal with. There's no crying in baseball, and no capos in bassball.

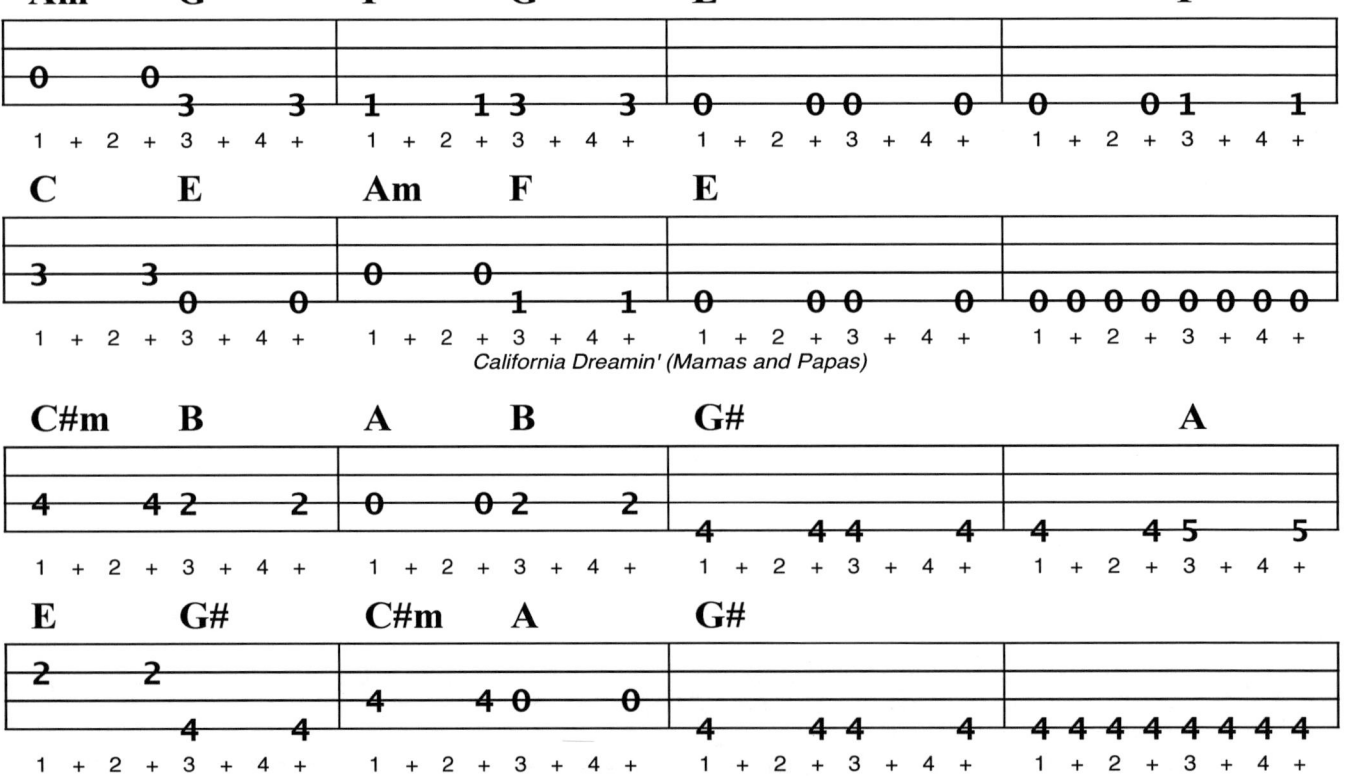
California Dreamin' (Mamas and Papas)

The Flamenco Chord Progression

I may be showing my ignorance here, but it seems to me that a lot of the flamenco music I've heard makes use of a variation of the above progression that extends one step farther down the scale to hit the **5 chord** before starting over from the top: **1m - 7 - 6 - 5**.

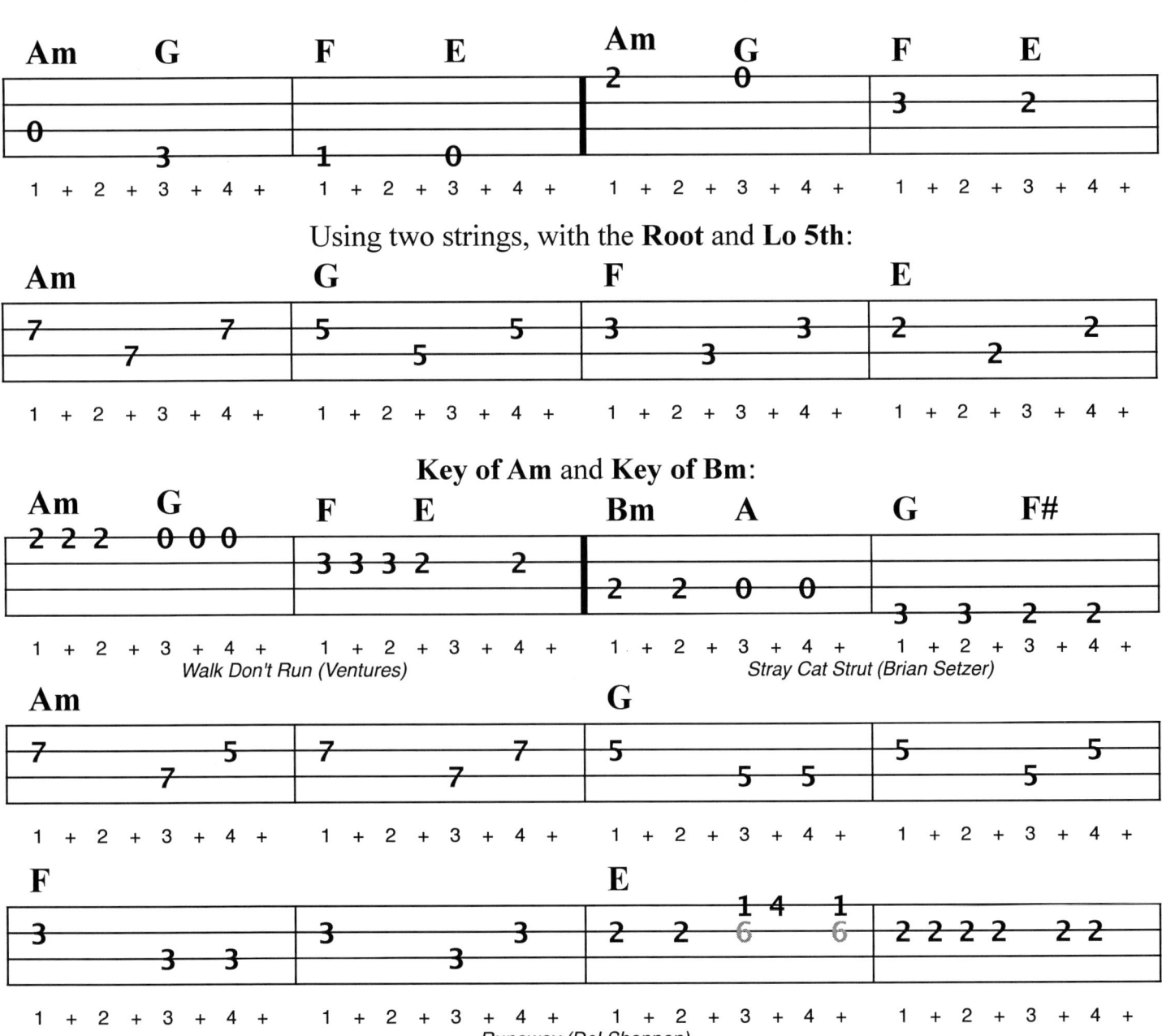

Clave Rhythm: The Bo Diddley Beat

One last thing to toss your way. We've used what I've called the *Half-Clave rhythm* a fair amount; in fact, it appears in that very last riff on the previous page. Well, here's the rest of the Clave pattern, the way Bo Diddley introduced it to American audiences in the 1950s in songs like "Bo Diddley," "I'm a Man" and "Mona". It's essentially 5 beats over 2 bars, and you can see it being done slightly differently in these 5 examples:

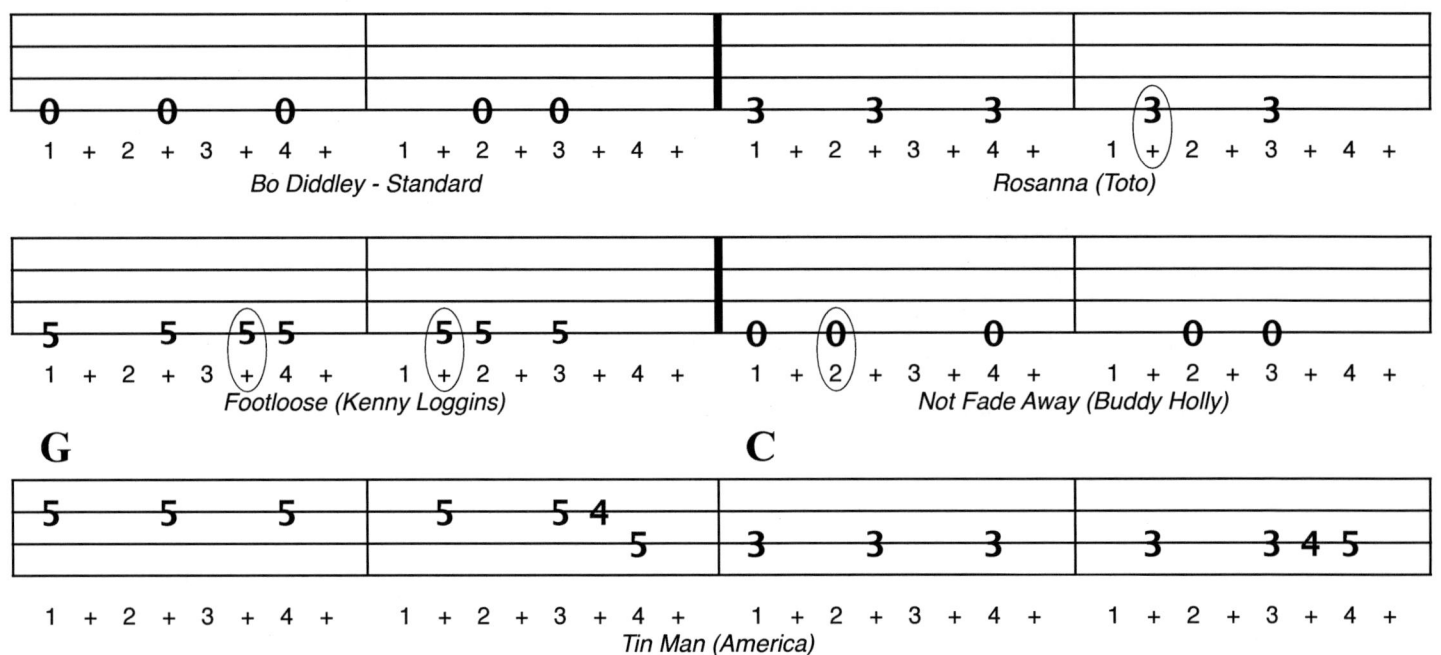

Parting Shot

If you've made it this far in the book, I'll eat my hat. But welcome! Here's a beauty. It's got the **1 - 4 - 5**s, the Jazz Turnaround (**F#m** to **B**), the **87654325**, and finishes up with the Rhythm Changes in **E**. Thanks for reading!